AMERICA'S WARS—WHY?

Man has always known war—a nation's history revolves around its battles. This book traces the involvement of the United States on the world's battlefields, from the American Revolution to the present conflict in Southeast Asia. Is there a pattern in the history of America's wars? Were they preventable? Why *did* America fight?

BOOKS BY ELINOR GOETTEL

AMERICA'S WARS – WHY?

by Elinor Goettel

Julian Messner New York

Published by Julian Messner
a division of Simon & Schuster, Inc.
1 West 39th Street, New York, N.Y. 10018
All Rights Reserved

My son Glenn wrote the first two pages of this book when he was fourteen years old.

Library of Congress Cataloging in Publication Data

Goettel, Elinor.
    America's wars—why?
    SUMMARY: Examines for recurring patterns the causes of United States involvement on the world's battlefields, from the Revolution to the war in Vietnam.
    Bibliography: p.
    1. United States—History, Military—Juvenile literature.
[1. United States—History, Military] I. Title.
E181.G6   973   72-1420
ISBN 0-671-32547-7
ISBN 0-671-32548-5 (lib. bdg.)
        Printed in the United States of America

Credits

All quotes in this book are documented. Unless otherwise indicated, they are taken from eyewitness accounts or contemporary newspapers.

" . . . It is my earnest hope that pondering upon the past may give guidance in days to come, enable a new generation to repair some of the errors of former years and thus govern, in accordance with the needs and glory of man, the awful unfolding scene of the future."

Winston Churchill

CONTENTS

Introduction

Central east Africa . . . 2,000,000 years before the birth of Christ . . .

The near-man slays an antelope. He gorges. Then he sleeps.

Dusk. The near-man awakens to the sound of teeth cracking bone. His prey is being usurped! Many times in the past has his prey been thus stolen by baboon, hyena and lion. Seizing his antelope horn, he rushes to drive off the intruder. Then he stops, astonished. The thief is not a baboon, hyena or lion. It is one of his own species.

The near-man hesitates for a moment, his small brain confused. Then he races forward, seizes his fellow man by the scalp and plunges the horn deep into the furred throat.

He has saved his catch.

A million and a half years later . . .

The meat-eaters gather at the foot of their mountain home to journey to the river for water. As they near their destination, they see that *they* are already there. *They* are cave dwellers, like themselves. They stand erect and make tools. But instead of fangs, they have blunt, grinding teeth. They are slower, less muscular. Their hands are not made for tearing flesh and breaking bone. They are the vegetable-eaters.

With a howl of rage, the meat-eaters charge to the banks of the river, hurling stones and brandishing their crude wooden spears. The vegetable-eaters flee toward the far end of the canyon. The meat-eaters pursue. They surround. They slaughter.

The river is now theirs.

Same valley . . . more than half a million years later . . .

The farmers tend their crops. Suddenly, from the surrounding forest, a hideous battle cry resounds. Warriors emerge from the trees, wielding great painted shields and long-bladed spears. They sweep through the fields, killing and burning. They leave, triumphant, returning to their village with ivory and slaves.

A good day's work!

Mankind has always known war. From the very beginning, man has fought against man. People banding together have found relative peace with each other under some kind of custom or law, but they have always waged war with strangers.

Tribes have fought against tribes, fiefdoms against fiefdoms, cities against cities, nations against nations.

For millions of years, people have accepted war as a part of life—like illness and pain and death.

Just as a plague could strike without warning, felling thousands and bringing untold grief, so could hordes of invaders suddenly sweep across a land. Or a monarch, playing for power, could conscript his helpless subjects and use them like pawns in a game of chess. The world has always been a lawless jungle where, as Matthew Arnold said, ignorant armies clash by night.

Even today, with the planet's very existence at stake, there is little recourse when nations disagree. Fear and distrust abound. The strong still tread on the weak. The "haves" stubbornly defend the status quo. The hydrogen bomb hangs like a sword of Damocles over the heads of all. Peace is a distant dream.

Many nations also face serious domestic unrest. While law and government appear to be war's best prevention, they are not an absolute guarantee of peace. Nations have been known to come apart at the seams. People sometimes rise against their established orders to wage hideous war until one side finally triumphs and either a new order is established (often as unjust as the old) or the insurgents are brutally crushed.

Thus, there are basically two kinds of war: those *between* organized societies, and those *within* an organized society. The second, while not as common as the first, is usually the most horrible.

The United States has experienced both. Indeed, its frightful Civil War was one of the bloodiest in the history of the world. Fought with unsurpassed hatred by the largest armies then ever known, it left open sores for over a hundred years.

One often hears that America has not experienced invasion since the War of 1812, but that is simply not true. During the Civil War the Southern states were invaded by enormous armies —the enemy, in every sense of the word. The people of Tennessee, Virginia, Georgia and South Carolina, in particular, experienced all the horrors of invasion—lawlessness, pillage and murder.

The war wrought terrible destruction. Homes were indiscriminately looted and burned. Food was confiscated. Huge areas were systematically put to the torch. Virginia's beautiful

Shenandoah Valley was devastated as General Philip Sheridan followed Grant's grim orders to so completely destroy that "crows flying over . . . will have to carry their provender with them." Grant even used the words "barren waste." Nothing was left for the women and children, the sick and the old.

The Southerners "regard us just as the Romans did the Goths," General William Sherman wrote his wife, "and the parallel is not unjust." This scrappy general, determined to "make Georgia howl," cut a swath of destruction sixty miles wide from Atlanta to the sea, leaving famine in his wake, and then unleashed his men on South Carolina. After they burned the city of Columbia to the ground, Sherman wrote, "Even if peace and prosperity soon return, not for a century can this city or state recover."

But before those areas lay open to invasion, men slugged it out on the battlefields, and there the slaughter was dreadful. The new Springfield rifles, with their improved firepower and deadly *Minié* bullets, were inflicting more damage than had ever been known before. Men fell dead by the thousands, while the wounded were so mangled that amputation was often the only hope of saving life.

And what a nightmare amputation was! In the crowded, filthy "hospitals," harassed doctors ("from whom our men had as much to fear as from their Northern enemies," according to one bitter Confederate officer) worked day and night, severing shattered limbs. Soldiers' memoirs repeatedly told of "bloody tables" and "heaps of feet, legs and arms." "As fast as one man was fixed up he was taken away and the doctor said, 'Next,' like a barber in a barber shop." "Horrors upon horrors," Mary Chestnut wrote in her diary after an afternoon of nursing.

"Want of organization, long rows of men dead and dying; awful smiles and awful sights."

The American Civil War was the first "modern" war, the first large-scale pitting of men against machines of destruction. Troops were forced to dig in, to seek cover—actions that had previously been considered cowardly. Leaders learned from terrible experience the futility of storming entrenchments. The Union general Ambrose Burnside received his painful education at Fredericksburg, where he poured his men against a killing fire from Marye's Heights and suffered 13,000 casualties in a few hours. General Grant got his lesson at Cold Harbor, where he lost 5,000 soldiers in eight minutes. And General Lee could never forget Pickett's charge at Gettysburg.

The European military observers surely absorbed these vivid lessons. Surely they reported that war had changed, that infantry could not be thrown against machines, that determination and bravery alone could no longer carry the day. But people forget, or refuse to learn, and in World War I, the ossified European generals made all the old mistakes.

The blind mass murder that was World War I killed almost three times as many soldiers as had all the major wars since 1790—a figure that ran into the millions. The war left seven million men disabled, their bodies so permanently broken that they were doomed to a hell on earth for the rest of their lives. And how could one begin to describe the suffering of the civilians? In Poland, after only a year and a half of war, it was reported that "one-third of a generation, the youngest, has practically ceased to exist due to famine, pestilence and disease."

On the western front, the war deadlocked along a battle line that stretched from the Alps to the English Channel. Two gigantic armies dug themselves into the ground and faced each other across a no-man's-land of shell holes and barbed wire. Despite the use of new and terrible weapons, which rained death on a scale never before envisioned, neither side could budge the other.

The generals did not know how to handle such a stalemate. They could think of nothing better than to throw their men against the entrenched enemy, in charge after futile charge. They repeatedly launched their monstrous offensives, feeding their troops into the enemy's machines, sacrificing hundreds of thousands of lives to gain ten feet here, five there.

For cannon fodder each nation, as always in war, selected its choicest men, sending youths who had not yet had a chance to live to die in a war they did not understand.

"I am young, I am twenty years old," stated the German hero in Erich Maria Remarque's classic *All Quiet on the Western Front*. "Yet I know nothing of life but despair, death, fear. . . . I see how peoples are set against one another, and in silence, unknowingly, foolishly, obediently, innocently slay one another."

Remarque's German soldiers, like people everywhere, wondered how wars got started in the first place:

" 'Mostly by one country badly offending another,' answers Albert.

"Then Tjaden pretends to be obtuse. 'A country? I don't follow. A mountain in Germany cannot offend a mountain in France. Or a river, or a wood, or a field of wheat.'

" '. . . I don't mean that at all. One people offends the other—'

" 'Then I haven't any business here at all,' replies Tjaden. 'I don't feel myself offended.' "

But when the attack came, it mattered little how one felt about the enemy. "We do not fight, we defend ourselves against annihilation," Remarque reported. "It is not against men that we fling our bombs, what do we know of men in this moment when Death with hands and helmets is hunting us down? . . . We crouch behind every . . . barrier of barbed-wire, and hurl heaps of explosives at the feet of the advancing enemy before we run . . . overwhelmed by this wave that bears us along, that fills us with ferocity, turning us into . . . murderers. . . . If your own father came over with them you would not hesitate to fling a bomb into him."

After only six months of war, casualties were already in the millions. "Down all the roads from the front . . . came back the tide of wounded," reported a British war correspondent, "wounded everywhere, maimed men at every junction; hospitals crowded with blind and dying and moaning men."

"We see men living with their skulls blown open," related Remarque. "We see soldiers run with thir two feet cut off, they stagger on their splintered stumps into the next shell-hole; a lance-corporal crawls a mile and a half on his hands dragging his smashed knee after him; another goes to the dressing-station and over his clasped hands bulge his intestines; we see men without mouths, without jaws, without faces; we find one man who has held the artery of his arm in his teeth for two hours in order not to bleed to death."

"Having despaired of living amid such horror," quietly reported a French priest, "we begged God . . . to let us be dead."

So terrible was World War I that most people thought the planet could not survive another such conflict. Yet only twenty-one years later a holocaust erupted beside which the slaughter of World War I paled almost to insignificance.

Germany had lost a million and a half men in World War I; in World War II, her battle deaths alone were three million, while no accurate figures are available for the hundreds of thousands of civilians who perished. People had long been haunted by Russia's incredible World War I losses: two million known dead, with another two million never accounted for. But Russia's World War II dead—soldier and civilian—are believed to have approached *twenty million*. And who could ever forget the six million Jewish men, women and children so heartlessly executed?

The individual tales of World War II comprise a monstrous horror story. Yet such hellishness has been present in all wars. Study each in detail, and the atrocities blend into one another. "If you have seen but one day of war," declared the Duke of Wellington, "you would pray God you might never see another."

No matter how small the war, how insignificant the casualties, the misery teems. The Spanish-American conflict, which cost fewer than four hundred American battle deaths, was so relatively painless that an American statesman could call it "a splendid little war." Yet "The procession is, indeed, terrible!" remembered a soldier who had fought at Santiago. "Men with arms in slings; men with bandaged legs and bloody faces . . . men staggering along unaided; men in litters, some groaning, some silent . . . some dead, some dying! . . . Ye Gods! It is raining lead! Men are dropping everywhere! . . . the slaughter is awful! . . . The bullets . . . are raining into our very faces. A soldier comes running up, and cries out, 'Lieutenant, we're shooting into our own men!' . . . Great is the confusion! How helpless, oh, how helpless we feel! Our men are being shot down under our very feet, and we, their officers, can do nothing for them."

The death of a man is the same, whether he be one of

hundreds or one of millions. "The man lives, he is strong, he is vital, every muscle in him is at its fullest tension when, suddenly 'chug' he is dead," wrote a Spanish-American war correspondent. "That 'chug' of bullets striking flesh is nearly always plainly audible."

"I heard somebody dying near me," reported Stephen Crane. "He was dying hard. . . . It took him a long time to die. . . . I thought this man would never die. I wanted him to die. Ultimately he died."

What is it all about, this senseless sacrifice of men, this cataclysmic way of solving national differences? If *people* can live in peace, then why can't nations? *Why* must there be war?

One of the strangest things about war is its appeal to the imagination, despite its very atrocity. Men hate war, and they love it. War may be hell, but it excites them. The songs and flags and trumpets, the rolling drums and marching feet, have stirred men's blood for centuries. Poets have long extolled "the rapture of the fight." Who is not touched by Kipling's noble tribute to the Fuzzie Wuzzies, who actually "broke the British square," or by Helen Gray Cone's proud description of Pickett's Virginians, "Peerless, fearless, an army's flower. . . . Marching lightly, that summer hour, To death and failure and fame forever"?

War has always been glorified. A nation's history revolves around its battles and victories. A nation's heritage is the heroes who have triumphed in its defense. A nation never forgets the man who says, "Damn the torpedoes, full speed ahead!" or "I only regret that I have but one life to give for my country."

Even the most avid opponents of war can testify to the intensity of war experience. Nothing can compare with the comradeships forged under fire, with the exhilarating sense of

purpose when people work together for "a cause that is just."
And who can deny that good sometimes comes out of war,
that wars have produced medical advances, for example, which
might otherwise never have occurred? With this in mind, perhaps it is even possible to understand Theodore Roosevelt's
incredible insistence, "This country *needs* a war!"

Few Americans would want to undo the results of the Revolution, when they gained their independence; the War of 1812,
when their bullied little nation earned the respect of the world;
or World War II, which put an end once and for all to the
horrors of Nazism (although, in the latter case, one might
logically ask why millions had to die to undo the work of
what was essentially *one man*).

The power of war's enchantment can be seen when veterans,
many of whom experienced worse horrors than Dante ever
imagined in hell, can look back on their war years with *nostal-
gia*. Listen to this Civil War soldier, a Southerner, who fought
from beginning to end under the most intolerable conditions,
including those last heartbreaking, starving, freezing months
in the trenches around Petersburg, and who tasted the bitter
gall of Appomattox:

> Who knows but it may be given to us, after this life, to
> meet again in the old quarters, to play chess and draughts
> . . . to fall in at the tap of the drum for drill and dress
> parade, and again to hastily don our war gear while the . . .
> long roll summons to battle? Who knows but again the
> old flags, ragged and torn, snapping in the wind, may face
> each other . . . while the cries of victory fill a summer day?
> And after the battle, then the slain and wounded will
> arise, and all will meet together under the two flags . . .

and there will be talking and laughter and cheers, and all will say: Did it not seem real? Was it not as in the old days?

Ah, how ugliness fades with the years! How easily people forget! Yet they do not really forget. It has always been this way—this love and this hatred for war.

Most people don't want war. But there are those in every society who do. There are the bored, who crave excitement; the naive, who have illusions of glory; the hateful, who need an outlet for their emotions; or simply the poor, the suffering and the downtrodden, who think that any change would be for the better.

Except for the blacks, who have been so shamefully oppressed that until recently they have had no effective voice in their government, Americans have been a happy people. Far removed from the squabbles of the Old World, insulated by two broad oceans, plentifully supplied with land and its riches, they were free for years to work and grow. War has almost always been an unwelcome interruption in their busy lives.

Why, then, did they fight? How did they get drawn into their many conflicts? Is there a pattern, some valuable clue, traceable in the history of American wars? Were those wars preventable, or were the problems actually beyond man's ability to resolve?

Let us examine this phenomenon of war. What, in each instance, finally prompted the American people to resort to arms and throw their young men into battle?

I

The American Revolution

America was born of war. She could not achieve her independence without it.

Yet most colonial Americans did not even want independence. They were devoted to their mother country. To the very end, most of them hoped that their problems could be resolved peacefully.

But England believed that the colonies existed solely for her benefit, and a parent can use a child for his own purposes for only so long. If the child is strong and healthy, he eventually wants a life of his own.

By 1775 the thirteen American colonies were no longer children; they were strapping young men. Stretching along the Atlantic coast from New England to Georgia and inland to the Appalachian Mountains, they comprised an area larger than that of most European countries. Their birth rate was enormous, their resources staggering.

Their people would never tolerate repression. They were a hearty breed, rugged and optimistic—and also "haughty and insolent, impatient of rule, disdaining subjection," according to one Englishman, who compared them unfavorably with the "pliant and submissive" inhabitants of India.

The rich and limitless land had made them that way; it offered incomparable opportunity to all. In Europe, the peasants were tied to their piece of earth, mired in poverty. But in America, a man could always move on and attain his goals. Submitting to a rigid monarch 3,000 miles across the sea made no sense on the American frontier, where every man was king.

Until 1763 Americans were the freest people on earth, enjoying all the rights of Englishmen without experiencing many of their burdens. Great Britain pursued a happy policy of "salutary neglect," and in the wild new land self-government flourished as it did nowhere in Europe.

Then, in 1763, Britain emerged triumphant from the Seven Years' War (in America, the "French and Indian War"), and nothing was ever the same again. Suddenly the owner of a vast world empire spanning four continents, England was faced with new administrative problems. Tight central control of all the colonies appeared to be called for. England had also piled up a staggering war debt, for which she wanted financial help from America. Hence the levying of taxes, the cracking down on smuggling, the quartering of troops in North America and, to prevent Indian troubles, a proclamation forbidding any settlement beyond the Appalachian Mountains. The dismayed American colonists refused to accept these unprecedented restrictions.

And there we have the basic human truth underlying the

American Revolution: No one who has ever tasted freedom will willingly surrender one iota of it.

Neither King George III nor any of his ministers had ever been to the New World. They had no concept of America's strength and spirit. They were astonished by the people's reaction to the new strictures—beginning with the Stamp Act in 1765.

The Stamp Act was Parliament's first attempt to levy a direct, internal tax on the colonists. It promised to be an irksome tax, affecting nearly every transaction "that can be thought of among a trading active people." The Americans were outraged at such an intrusion into their domestic affairs.

What, they thought in horror, might come next? If the British could tax paper, then they might tax merchandise, land, crops, livestock—even windows and hearths, as they did in Ireland! They might try to establish a state church and tithe the people, as they did in England! They might draft colonists into the British Army! The motto *Principiis Obsta*—"Take a stand at the start"—was intuitively followed by the colonists.

Their "stand" was immediate and explosive—from the rough young burgess (Patrick Henry) in Williamsburg, Virginia, who dared to shout, "Tarquin and Caesar each had his Brutus, Charles the First his Cromwell, and George the Third . . . [cries of "Treason!"] may profit by their example"; to the Virginia Resolves, which insisted that a people could not be taxed without their consent; and even to the organization of the "Sons of Liberty," secret groups of radical intellectuals like Samuel Adams of Massachusetts, who urged the people to "fight up to their knees in blood" if necessary, even though the colonies be turned into "a most doleful scene of outrage, violence, desolation and slaughter."

When the Royal Stamp Officers were appointed, riots erupted

throughout the land. The Stamp Officers were hanged in effigy, their homes ransacked and burned and they themselves so roughly manhandled that one and all requested "the liberty of being excused" from their duties.

"I did not know whether I should have escaped from this Mob with my life," the New Hampshire Stamp Officer tremblingly reported, "as some were for Cutting off my head, others for Cutting off my ears and sending them home with my Commission."

Boston experienced the worst riot in its history, while in New York a howling mob of thousands beseiged the little fort at the Battery, sending the governor in terror-stricken flight to a British warship. The rabble then marched up Broadway to the home of an officer who had threatened to "cram the Stamps down the People's Throats" with his sword. They wrecked his furniture and his china, uprooted his garden, burned his library, helped themselves to his liquor and left carrying one of his curtains as a banner.

The British were aghast. They could not understand such behavior over "a few stamps." The colonist "must be the veriest beggars in the world," one Londoner remarked, "if such inconsiderable duties appear to be intollerable burthens in their eyes."

Not all Englishmen were blind to the real issues. A liberal minority actually sympathized with the colonists. William Pitt was moved to pronounce his famous "I rejoice that America has resisted," while Edmund Burke clearly understood that "this fierce spirit of liberty is stronger in the English colonies than in any other people on earth."

The Stamp Act obviously could not be enforced. Parliament finally repealed it and tried another approach. Since the Americans had objected to a "direct, internal tax," Parliament tried an "external" one: the levying of duties on certain English imports—surely acceptable, since the Americans had never questioned Parliament's right to regulate trade.

Ah, but the free-thinking colonists had no intention of relinquishing their "right" to tax themselves. They decided that the new duties were "illegal," since their intention was clearly to raise revenue rather than regulate trade. But this time they behaved like "dutiful children who have received unmerited blows from a beloved parent," in the words of John Dickinson, who advised in his *Letters of a Pennsylvania Farmer:* "Let us complain to the parent; but let our complaints speak at the same time the language of our affection and veneration."

Massachusetts accordingly issued a circular letter to her sister colonies, suggesting that "unified and dutiful supplications" be sent to "our most gracious sovereign," which, it was hoped, would meet with his "royal and favorable acceptance."

This specter of unified action brought out the beast in the British. They saw the mild Massachusetts epistle as "little better than an incentive to Rebellion." Massachusetts, they said, was acting "in the Stile of a ruling and Sovereign Nation, who acknowledges no Dependence." Foolishly they ordered the Massachusetts Assembly to rescind its letter upon pain of dismissal.

What could that proud body do but refuse and be dismissed?

All the colonial assemblies were now threatened with dismissal if they supported the Massachusetts letter. To the spunky Americans, this was "the most daring insult that ever was offered to any free legislature."

Up and down the country colonial assemblies eagerly approved the Massachusetts letter, and were promptly dissolved. When the Virginia House of Burgesses was dismissed, one member, the dignified George Washington, was angry enough to suggest resorting to arms to defend those freedoms "which we have derived from our ancestors."

Colony after colony joined a great Non-Importation Movement, agreeing to "Eat nothing, drink nothing, wear nothing imported from Great Britain" and to "buy American."

Men scorned English toddies for local ciders and whiskeys. Physicians looked to native herbs for their medicines. Women returned to the spinning wheels. New factories started operation.

"One Spirit animates all America," a Massachusetts citizen happily wrote. "And both the *justice* and *importance* of the cause is so plain, that to *quench* the spirit, *all the colonies* must be absolutely destroyed."

The boycott worked. Great Britain felt it. After terrific pressure from afflicted merchants, Parliament finally repealed the duties—but retained the tax on tea as a matter of principle.

Things might then have returned to normal had not the deadly cycle already begun. As with many wars, one incident would lead to another, until at last there was no turning back.

Rampaging mobs in Boston protesting the import duties had already prompted the garrisoning of that city by 4,000 British soldiers—nearly one for every four inhabitants. Such a situation was intolerable ("a hostile invasion," in the opinion of the Virginia burgesses).

Indignant citizens inevitably taunted the ever-present "Lobster Backs." Little boys pelted them with stones and snowballs. A crowd of ruffians harassed the sentry at the Old State House one cold March night, and when the main guard hurried out to support the hapless man, the mob grew larger and more threatening. Finally some poor redcoat lost control and fired into the crowd, killing five men and giving Samuel Adams all the ammunition he needed to create a hallowed "Boston Massacre" and turn the dead hoodlums into innocent martyrs.

The tax that Parliament retained on tea led indirectly to the Boston Tea Party, when 150 Bostonians, thinly disguised as Mohawk Indians, forcibly boarded three British ships and dumped 342 chests of precious tea into the harbor while thousands stood on the dock and cheered.

The Boston Tea Party, in turn, led to fatal harsh reprisals, for in England it was the last straw, uniting public opinion almost solidly against the colonists. The British felt that they had been superhumanly patient with their naughty child; it was time to bring out the rod—the worst possible approach to take with the high-spirited Americans but an understandable one, for throughout history few people have had the patience or the wisdom to sift to the actual issues beneath the ugly surface of rioting. The usual human reaction is to repress and punish. How difficult it is for us, even today, to appreciate Edmund Burke's brilliant thought, "Freedom . . . is the cure of anarchy!"

Boston had misbehaved, and Boston had to be punished. In the spring of 1774, Parliament passed what came to be known as the Coercive Acts—acts that led directly to the calling of a Continental Congress and, finally, to Lexington and Concord.

The Coercive Acts canceled all self-government in Massachusetts; forced private citizens to quarter British soldiers, who were pouring into Boston by the thousands; and—most drastic of all—closed the port of Boston, destroying the city's livelihood, throwing men out of work, severing the inhabitants from virtually all provisions and threatening them with ruin and starvation.

Although these acts were directed at Massachusetts, every

colony felt threatened. As the Virginia burgesses resolved, "An attack made on one of our sister Colonies . . . is an attack on all British America." The colonists could not, in the words of George Washington, "supinely sit and see one province after another fall a prey to despotism."

The child had to rebel against the parent, who, in the words of an irate citizen, was trying to "crush" his "native talents" and keep him "in a constant state of inferiority."

Benjamin Franklin, in London, tried to tell the British that they could not repress the colonies. America's potential was so enormous, he insisted, that the sheer momentum of her growth would eventually sweep aside all restrictions. If she were allowed to progress unhampered, she would someday be a magnificent feather in Britain's cap. Together, America and Great Britain could "awe the world."

But few people can envision what they have never known. A relationship of equals, such as England now enjoys in her Commonwealth, was too advanced an idea for 1774. Most Englishmen could only look back, to the days of Rome, and see their country as a great sun forever orbited by inferior satellites serving her interests. It was either that or, as one perplexed Englishman put it, "We may just as well give up all ideas of having colonies at all."

"Great Britain is *determined* upon her system," a friend tried to warn John Adams.

"I know that Great Britain is determined in her system, and that very determination determined me on mine," replied the dour Massachusetts lawyer. "I have passed the Rubicon; swim or sink, live or die, survive or perish with my country—that is my unalterable determination."

When men are willing to die for a cause, they are irresistible.

And when an irresistible force meets an immovable object, the result is very often war.

Boston was the powder keg. That city, under the heavy military occupation of General Thomas Gage, was a fortress island in a growing sea of rebellion. Just outside the city limits, out of range of the British cannon, farmers were drilling, making gunpowder and molding bullets, grimly determined to resist any British invasion of their land.

Repeal the Coercive Acts, Benjamin Franklin frantically advised the British Government. Repeal the Coercive Acts and remove the army from Boston, or "even God Almighty" will not effect a reconciliation.

"It is not yet too late to accommodate the dispute," Dr. Joseph Warren of Massachusetts wrote a friend in London. "But if once General Gage should lead his troops into the country, with design to enforce the late Acts of Parliament, Great Britain may take her leave . . . of all America."

General Gage received his orders that spring: arrest the Massachusetts revolutionaries.

All Americans know what happened when General Gage sent his troops into the Massachusetts countryside: the midnight ride of Paul Revere to sound the long-expected alarm; the frantic tolling of the church bells to summon the men from their beds, men who had promised to spring to arms at a minute's notice; and the long scarlet columns filing into Lexington at dawn, tootling "Yankee Doodle Dandy" on their fifes and finding some seventy proud villagers awaiting them in battle formation on the misty green.

"Stand your ground," the Massachusetts commander, Jonas Parker, told his men. "Don't fire unless fired upon. But if they mean to have a war, let it begin here."

The British: "Disperse, ye rebels, disperse! Lay down your arms!"

The Americans, surrounded by superior numbers, fell away, and in the confusion a shot—whose?—more shots, muskets blazing, bayonets flashing, Americans breaking for cover, followed by British bullets as long as they were within range. When the heavy smoke cleared, eight villagers were dead or dying—including Jonas Parker, gored by a bayonet while he was attempting to reload.

The British then proceeded to Concord, where there was a large store of colonial arms. Meanwhile, the "Minutemen" continued converging from every town and hamlet within a tremendous radius. While the redcoats were destroying what military supplies the Concord patriots had not had time to hide, some 350 Minutemen surprised a British covering party at the crude North Bridge and there, "their flags to April's breeze unfurl'd," they stood and "fired the shot heard round the world."

From then on, it was a nightmare for the British. The Americans didn't stop coming—amateur soldiers, ordinary citizens answering a call, pouring in from as far away as Connecticut and New Hampshire. The British had to run a terrible gauntlet, "a Veritable Furnass of Musquetry," from Concord back down the narrow road to Boston, peppered by fire every step of the way. The furious Americans tormented them like bees— shooting Indian-style from behind trees, barns, wood piles or stone walls and picking them off like woodcocks or grouse. The fighting became bitter as British flankers, thrown out to protect the column, engaged the patriots, often in hand-to-hand clashes. Hundreds more patriots came up, and the desperate British altered their route, hurrying not for Boston, but for

Charlestown peninsula. They finally reached it just after sunset, safe at last under the guns of the Royal Navy. It was "a most vigorous retreat," in the words of Edmund Burke to Parliament, "twenty miles in three hours—scarce to be paralleled in history."

Up swarmed the Americans—polyglot, disorganized, untrained, but 15,000 strong—to surround the 6,000 hapless British troops in Boston, imprisoning them in the city they had so arrogantly occupied. War had begun.

The electrifying news spread through the colonies by fast post riders, creating frenzied excitement everywhere. "Last Wednesday, the 19th of April," reported the Salem *Essex Gazette,* "the troops of his *Britannick* Majesty commenced Hostilities upon the People of this Province. . . . We are involved in all the Horrors of a civil War. . . . "

So it had come to civil war, with Englishmen against colonial Englishmen—"a Brother's Sword," in the words of George Washington, "sheathed in a Brother's Breast."

Rebellion sprung up all over. In Virginia, the royal governor made the mistake of seizing the colony's powder supply, and within hours an indignant crowd prepared to storm his palace. He subsequently fled to a British warship, from which he periodically shelled the coastal towns. In upper New York state, Ethan Allen and his Green Mountain Boys seized Fort Ticonderoga from the sleeping British garrison "in the name of the great Jehovah and the Continental Congress." Everywhere, royal officials fled to England, leaving the colonists to set up what became in fact their state governments.

The Second Continental Congress made one last try for peace—the Olive Branch Petition, begging the King to stop the war, repeal the Coercive Acts and bring about a "happy and permanent reconciliation." But by then, near Boston, one of the bloodiest battles of the eighteenth century had already been fought—Bunker Hill, in which the British suffered 40 per cent casualties and the Americans displayed "a spirit and conduct against us, they never shewed against the French," according to General Gage, who was shocked at their "Rage and Enthusiasm, as great as ever People were possessed of."

If there had been any doubt in King George's mind before— and there probably wasn't—Bunker Hill certainly dispelled it.

On August 23, 1775, he proclaimed the existence of a general rebellion "open and avowed," saying that "utmost endeavors" should be made to "suppress such rebellion, and to bring the traitors to justice."

Yet almost a year passed before the colonists could bring themselves to declare their independence. How difficult it was to sever "that union which has so long and so happily subsisted." How risky to sail into the unknown! Could Americans actually prevail over the mightiest nation on earth? Even so, might they not eventually fall apart, fight among themselves, fall prey to France or Spain? "The Novelty . . . deters some," wrote Benjamin Franklin, "the Doubt of Success, others, the vain Hope of Reconciliation, many. But our Enemies continually . . . remove these Obstacles."

Indeed, the obvious determination of the British to crush the rebellion finally left the Americans no choice. This was cogently pointed out to them in a remarkable pamphlet that appeared early in 1776, calling for a declaration of independence on the grounds that the events at Lexington and Concord had ended all possibility of reconciliation. Americans could no longer "love, honor and faithfully serve the power that hath carried fire and sword into the land."

This pamphlet, entitled *Common Sense* and written by an English ne'er-do-well named Thomas Paine who had lived in the colonies only two years, had a tremendous impact. Its compelling logic and passionate prose wrought "a powerful change in the minds of many men," according to George Washington, who, until he read it, had been toasting the King nightly at dinner.

Paine maintained that it was "something absurd" for "a Continent to be perpetually governed by an island." He insisted that " 'TIS TIME TO PART."

What freedom-loving American could do otherwise? "O! ye that dare oppose not only the tyranny but the tyrant, stand forth! Every spot of the old world is overrun with oppression. Freedom hath been hunted round the globe. Asia and Africa have long expelled her. Europe regards her like a stranger, and England hath given her warning to depart. O! receive the fugitive and prepare in time an asylum for mankind."

Paine declared that "the cause of America is in a great measure the cause of all mankind." Indeed, "The Sun never shined on a cause of greater worth."

Here was the beginning of the "missionary complex" destined to influence U.S. foreign policy for endless generations to come—the feeling that Americans had a sacred mission: in the words of John Adams, "the emancipation of the slavish part of mankind." As Benjamin Rush later explained, "I was constantly animated by a belief that I was acting for the benefit of the whole world, and of future ages."

Led by young, shy Thomas Jefferson, Americans proceeded to denounce tyranny as unbearable *anywhere*. In one of the greatest human documents ever written, they boldly asserted: "We hold these truths to be self-evident, that all men are created equal, that they are endowed by their creator with certain unalienable Rights, that among these are Life, Liberty, and the Pursuit of Happiness." On these principles, idealistic beyond imagination, they would actually attempt to found a nation.

The time had come to declare that the thirteen separate colonies were, "and of right, ought to be, free and independent states." Incredible that those people, proud Englishmen for 175 golden years, thriving and prospering beyond compare under British rule, had come to such a pass. "We might have been a free and a great people together," Thomas Jefferson reflected sadly. The problems were so solvable, the issue so simple—in the words of a Continental soldier some sixty-five years after the event: "We always had governed ourselves, and we always meant to. They didn't mean we should."

The American Revolution was the first successful large-scale colonial uprising in history. It profoundly affected the course of mandkind, forcing liberal reforms in England and inspiring the French Revolution, all the South American revolts and even the independence movements in Africa and Asia two centuries later.

Still it was war—bringing "the Sickness, the Wounds, the Death of Thousands; the Desolation of Provinces; the Waste of the Human Species; the Mourning of Parents; the Cries and Tears of Widows and Orphans."

Could it have been avoided?

Yes, if the Americans had tamely submitted. But they deeply felt, along with Thomas Jefferson, that "Honour, justice, and humanity" forbade such a capitulation.

As Patrick Henry so eloquently put it, "Is life so dear, or

peace so sweet, as to be purchased at the price of chains and slavery? Forbid it, almighty God!"

But should the Americans have been more patient? Should they have bided their time, working for their goals, always within the British Empire, never resorting to revolution?

The colonists felt that time was of the essence. In the words of John Adams, "a constitution of government, once changed from freedom, can never be restored. Liberty, once lost, is lost forever." *Principiis Obsta*—"Take a stand at the start!" With Thomas Jefferson, they were "with one mind resolved to die free men rather than live slaves."

While it is true that Great Britain eventually abandoned her colonial system in favor of a great commonwealth of nations, did it not take the traumatic loss of her thirteen most prized colonies to start her in that direction?

What of the rabble rousers who stirred the people to acts of violence, like the Stamp Act riots and the Boston Tea Party? Didn't they contribute immensely to the deadly cycle that led to war? They certainly did. People, left alone, tend to be politically lethargic. They never rise to revolution without skillful leadership. However, that leadership will not succeed without fertile soil.

War came because the British chose a policy of suppression. Had they been willing to negotiate, then all the inflammatory words of Patrick Henry and Thomas Paine and all the skillful propagandizing by men like Samuel Adams would have come to naught.

The British should have tried to understand their subjects. When ordinary citizens—farmers, lawyers, merchants, cobblers—rise up against a professional army, then something is obviously wrong. England, the most democratic nation on earth, had created her own monster. Only from *her* colonies could such an epochal revolution have come. As always, the fruit had not fallen far from the tree.

This failure to understand the people involved is almost always found in preludes to war. How significant it now seems that the first minister, Lord North, fell asleep in Parliament whenever the "American problem" was discussed! Had he stayed awake, might he not have gained some valuable insight? Might he not at least have grasped the military aspects and realized that the British were biting off more than they would be able to chew?

When the British finally realized that they had initiated a major undertaking, they lost all heart for it. They could not summon the will to use the amount of force that was required. The fighting threatened to be endless, bcause the American army, despite continual defeats, refused to be defeated.

That volunteer "rabble in arms"—a motley collection of bounty hunters, renegades and patriots who came and went— was singularly disorganized: poorly armed, undisciplined, underfed, even unpaid. But it had several great advantages. Its soldiers were superb marksmen, fighting defensively on home soil. And they had an indomitable leader in George Washington, who displayed unswerving courage and determination in the face of continual catastrophe.

General Washington never left his post at the helm. With unshakable dignity, he weathered intrigue, treason and Congressional neglect, rallied his men, endured untold hardship and managed at all times to keep an army in the field— bedraggled, often pathetically small, but always an armed symbol of independence.

Washington was no genius, and he made many mistakes. But

he was shrewd, relentless, unconquerable—an "old fox" who, six and a half years after Lexington and Concord, finally brought his battered ship home, towing—thanks to French intervention—the greatest prize of war: victory.

Yorktown, October, 1781 . . . The defeated British, tears in their eyes, their fifes tootling "The World Turned Upside Down," marched between lines of French and American soldiers to lay down their arms.

As James Russell Lowell would later write:

> *They came three thousand miles and died*
> *To keep the Past upon its throne;*
> *Unheard beyond the ocean tide,*
> *Their English mother made her moan.*

"O God! It is all over! It is all over!" Lord North exclaimed again and again.

The formal treaty was signed in Paris on September 3, 1783. Great Britain surrendered the heart of her empire, recognizing thirteen free and independent states extending north to the Great Lakes and west to the Mississippi River.

A great principle had triumphed over an old-fashioned concept of government. Now, out of the pain of war, would be born a jewel—a republic, a dream worth fighting and dying for.

II

The War of 1812

The new nation thrived, even while Europe underwent a tremendous upheaval. In France, the peasants rose in arms, murdered their king and queen, instituted a bloody Reign of Terror and then attempted to extend their revolution to neighboring countries. The result, as so often is the case when the status quo is threatened, was war—a war over the entire continent which persisted, with one brief respite, for twenty-six years.

The enterprising Americans were quick to take advantage of a Europe in arms. They picked up England's peacetime trade. While England and France grappled to the death, American foreign commerce tripled. New England became one of the wealthiest sections on the globe, her shipyards resounding to the sounds of hammer and saw as ship after ship rolled down the ways to the sea. The Stars and Stripes was seen in ports all over the world, flying from the masts of beautifully built, capacious vessels, whose crews were hard-working, high-spirited and well treated.

Meanwhile, Napoleon, the tiger, conquered all of Europe. England, the shark, triumphed at sea. Neither the tiger nor the shark could quite get at the other. Desperate, England tried to strangle France by severing her lifeline—in a series of Orders-in-Council, she banned trade with the entire European continent. Napoleon frantically struck back, prohibiting trade with England. The United States, the world's largest neutral carrier, was caught right in the middle.

And here lay the problem: a neutral nation trying to survive in a world at war—an ominous preview of the circumstances that would bring the United States into two world wars one century later. But in 1812, America was inconsequential, a small power, easily depredated.

English frigates captured hundreds of American cargo ships on the mere presumption that they were heading for French destinations. And Napoleon's harbor patrols seized countless American vessels on the presumption that they had visited a British port. The loss in American ships, crews and goods was enormous.

Since England had the navy, she inflicted the greatest damage. Furthermore, she added insult to injury with her abominable practice of impressment: stopping American cargo ships on the high seas and kidnaping members of their crews.

"We are only retrieving our deserters," British officials insisted when the United States angrily protested each incident of impressment. This was essentially true. Sailors were deserting the "floating hells" of the Royal Navy by the thousands, finding a haven in the far more humane American merchant marine. But in the process of retrieving their hapless deserters, the British were seizing many native-born Americans.

A crisis came in June, 1807, when the British stopped an American *war*ship in *American* waters and removed four of her crew. This was unprecedented. In an age when "honor" meant everything, such an insult to a country's navy was unforgivable. Even officials in London were shaken when they learned how far their admiralty had gone.

The victim was the proud man-of-war *Chesapeake*. Soon after she had put to sea from Hampton Roads, Virginia, the H.M.S. *Leopard* had closed on her and demanded permission to search for British deserters believed to be on board. When the *Chesapeake* refused, as any self-respecting warship would, the *Leopard* blasted her at close range, shattering her deck and causing twenty-one casualties. The Americans tried to fight back, but they were unprepared: many of their guns were not yet rigged, and most did not even have firing matches. It was a humiliating defeat. The sailors had to stand by, apoplectic with rage, while the British seized four of their crewmen— three of whom were native-born Americans.

The nation was outraged. Men fought personal duels over far less than this. Mass indignation meetings were held from Boston to Charleston. "It's bad enough for Americans to be constantly hauled off into slavery," people cried, "but when this happens under *American guns,* then we've got to act!" Cries of "Revenge!" and "Redeem our national honor!" rang through the land, as even the most conservative newspapers called for war.

Many leaders would have bowed to such pressure, but Thomas Jefferson was at the helm, and he was gifted with rare vision, patience and resolution. He had no intention of fighting over a shallow principle like "national honor." It would be better for Americans to feel briefly humiliated, he reasoned, than to suffer the horrors of an unnecessary war.

In an age when war was the accepted method of resolving national differences, this lanky, sandy-haired President loathed the very idea. He was a farmer, and his approach to people was agricultural: provide the proper climate and let them *grow*. The butchery of men in battle appalled him, while the repressive by-products of war—heavy taxes, a tremendous army and a too-powerful government—violated his most basic beliefs. Besides, another war with England made little sense to him. "No two countries on earth have so many points in common," he once wrote. "Their rulers must be great bunglers, indeed, if with such dispositions they break asunder."

He had to admit, however, that the British had acted outrageously, that they had "touched a chord which vibrates every heart." He dispatched a ship to England with a stern demand for the return of the seized Americans and the complete cessation of impressment.

Four years later, after endless negotiations, the British finally paid meager reparations and returned two of the four crewmen. By then, the other two were dead—one had been hanged from the yardarm of a ship; the other had succumbed to disease. Thus the *Chesapeake* affair remained an open sore for years.

While it festered, Jefferson strove mightily to keep his country out of war. Since it had become almost suicidal for Americans to trade anywhere, he resorted to one of the most extreme measures in American history: he forbade all trade everywhere! Henceforth, American ships would stay in port. There would be no more incidents, no war.

Merchants were aghast. Their livelihoods depended on that trade, however risky it might be. "God knows what all this means," a New York Congressman cried. "All our surplus produce will rot on our hands!"

But Jefferson insisted that if England were denied the American market, she might be forced to lift her bans on American trade with Europe. "I believe we have in our hands the means of peaceable coercion," he explained. The idea of substituting economic pressure for war fascinated him. His Embargo Act of 1807 was a noble, unprecedented attempt to find a peaceful alternative to war.

It brought disaster. The nation's economy skidded to a halt. Goods rotted on the wharves. Thousands of unemployed sailors, desperate from starvation, rioted in the streets. Depression spread over the land like a plague. Merchants went bankrupt. In the South, cotton remained unpicked in the fields; tobacco was given away.

Southerners and Westerners remained loyal to Jefferson despite catastrophe, but New Englanders were enraged. "If this is an alternative to war," they cried, "then for God's sake, let us have war!"

From New Hampshire came a quickly popular song:

> *Our ships all in motion once whitened the ocean;*
> *They sailed and returned with a cargo.*
> *Now doomed to decay, they are fallen aprey*
> *To Jefferson, worms, and EMBARGO!"*

"Let every man who holds the name of America dear to him put this accursed thing—the Embargo—from him!" cried a leaflet distributed in Newburyport. "Be resolute; act like the sons of liberty!"

People openly flouted the law. Ships secretly sailed for the West Indies. Smuggling over the Canadian border became big business. Courts refused to prosecute violators.

Jefferson should have seen the writing on the wall, but he was determined to give the experiment a fair trial, "so that on future occasions our legislators may know how far they may count on it." He strengthened the Embargo enforcement, dispatching Federal patrols to police the waterfronts.

The terrible winter gave way to spring, the spring to summer and the summer to fall, and so rebellious were the people in their misery that Jefferson, who saw no alternative except war, resorted to a virtual economic dictatorship to sustain his Embargo. But the people wouldn't stand for it. New Englanders mobilized in outrage, preparing to secede from the Union. "It is better to suffer the amputation of a limb than to lose the whole body," they cried.

Jefferson finally had to admit defeat. His staunch attempts to avoid a foreign war had led his people to the brink of civil war. Sadly, he asked Congress to rescind the Embargo. In later years he conceded that it had been costlier than war.

But he had won precious time, and it could have paid great dividends. His successor, the timid James Madison, with the wrinkled, "mean-looking" face and a queue "no bigger than a pipestem," picked up where Jefferson had left off, determined to achieve "peace if at all possible," but willing to accept "war rather than submission."

The situation Madison inherited was dreadful. Besides the domestic woes—New England was still threatening secession—conditions abroad were exactly as they had been before the Embargo: impossible.

The scholarly Madison did his best. He toiled day and night, using every diplomatic ploy in the books. He attempted playing off one belligerent against the other. He tried banning trade with both belligerents. Then he tried trading with both while offering inducements to each to suspend its restrictions. Nothing worked.

He seemed to have no bargaining power. The English did not want the competition of American ships bustling all over the Atlantic again. And the ruthless Napoleon, whose foreign minister told him that America was a "giant without bones," was bolstering his wobbly treasury by seizing every American vessel that entered a continental port.

In desperation Madison finally decided that Napoleon (who could not be trusted) was going to lift his restrictions. Or perhaps Madison decided to *pretend* that he thought so in order to prompt favorable action from England. In any event, the result was a fatal decision to cooperate with Napoleon and ban all trade with England.

The English were so furious that they dispatched several warships to patrol the American coast. These ships blockaded New York harbor and impressed seamen at will, sometimes within sight of the shore—an intolerable situation which led to a terrific gun battle one dark night between the U.S.S. *President* and the H.M.S. *Little Belt*. The *Little Belt,* severely damaged, limped off to Nova Scotia with nine dead and twenty-three wounded.

This naval victory thrilled Americans. At long last, after years of humiliation, they had fought back! The *Chesapeake* had finally been avenged!

Excitement was especially great on the frontier, where self-respecting men did not allow themselves to be pushed around. If England was seizing American ships and kidnaping American men, then Americans should fight! "I am for resistance by the sword!" cried Henry Clay of Kentucky. Like King George III's reaction to the "Savages of America," this approach was based on emotion, not—as is so essential if war is to be avoided —on reality.

But enough Americans shared these feelings to stage a spectacular revolt at the polls. In the 1810-11 Congressional elections, they swept almost half of the incumbents out of Congress, replacing them with young, vigorous men who promised action.

The fateful Twelfth Congress convened in November, 1811. It contained more Westerners than ever before. The nation's population was moving so steadily that the balance of power had finally shifted from the sophisticated east. Now the simple, hot-blooded frontiersmen, supported by the agrarian Southerners, could have an effective voice in the government.

Thomas Jefferson would have kept these "Buckskin Boys" (or "War Hawks," as they called themselves) in harness. But James Madison, brilliant though he was, lacked the executive ability to control them. As even Jefferson would later admit, "Alas, he [Madison] could never in his life stand up against strenuous opposition!"

For the first time the leadership of the country passed to Congress. The War Hawks grabbed the reins and galloped toward war, driving the helpless President like "chaff before the wind."

Fiery young Henry Clay, the new Speaker of the House of Representatives, became the "boy dictator" of Congress, dislodging the "old fogeys" from all the key committees, replacing them with fellow War Hawks and—following his strategy "Decide quickly and never give the reasons for your decision" —gaveling all war measures through.

"Mark my words," gasped Congressman John Randolph, a

peace advocate, "we shall have war before the end of the session."

But war with whom? Napoleon, despite his "cooperation," was seizing more American ships than the British. "The Devil himself could not tell which government, England or France, is the more wicked," declared Congressman Nathaniel Macon.

But the Westerners knew whom they wanted to fight. They sympathized with the "democratic" French and hated the haughty British, whom, among other things, they blamed for their Indian troubles.

It was true that in past years the British had inspired many of the Indian attacks on the American frontier. While they no longer directly initiated such acts, they were, nevertheless, actively cultivating the Indians as essential allies in case of war.

Hence the Americans thought that the British were behind every hostile Indian move. Rumors abounded that the British were arming the Indians; they were about to give the signal for a general massacre. Westerners lived in a state of continual fear.

In 1811, a powerful encampment of Indian braves sprang up on the Tippecanoe River in western Indiana, and that summer marauding parties roamed south, burning cabins, stealing horses and killing settlers. William Henry Harrison, governor of the Indiana territory, led a force of outraged citizens up the wild Wabash valley to engage them. When they neared Tippecanoe, the Indians met them, insisting, "We don't want to fight. Our leader will see you tomorrow in peace."

The Americans camped on an oak-covered ridge, and while they slept on that cold, wet night, the Indians launched a surprise attack, charging from two different directions. Savage hand-to-hand fighting ensued in the darkness and the rain.

Sixty-one Americans were killed before the Indians were finally driven off.

The next day the outraged Americans entered deserted Tippecanoe, where they found English-made arms and ammunition—all the evidence they needed to pin the deed on the hated British.

"BRITISH—SAVAGE WAR!" cried the frontier newspapers. "THE BLOW IS STRUCK!"

Westerners were now convinced that they would never be safe until the British were driven from the continent.

And what would the Americans gain when that happened? *Canada!* All that fertile land, believed to be so much more desirable than the timberless Great Plains! The War Hawks' mouths watered. Canada appeared to be theirs for the taking!

"The militia of Kentucky alone are competent to place Montreal and Upper Canada at your feet," was Henry Clay's opinion. "I am not for stopping at Quebec or anywhere else. I would take the entire continent!"

Spurred by the "battle" of Tippecanoe and a frank desire for Canada (two of the oldest spurs to war: revenge and greed), the Twelfth Congress passed a resolution "in favor of war, at a given period," which many people thought was an actual declaration.

The Federalists (members of the opposition party) were horrified. Most of them came from the Northeastern states—merchant territory, where men made their living by trading with England. The last thing they wanted was war with her.

"A scuffle and scramble for plunder!" charged the vinegary John Randolph, deploring the fact that he was continually hearing but one word, "like the whippoorwill, but one eternal, monotonous tone—Canada! Canada! Canada!"

"Where are your armies, your navy?" asked the sensible Congressman Hermanus Bleecker of New York. "Have you money?"

But the War Hawks couldn't be bothered with details. Along the frontier, from Vermont's green mountains to Kentucky's blue grass and Georgia's wild uplands, men who had never seen the ocean were crying, "Free Trade and Sailors' Rights!" These Westerners were determined to "Avenge the blood spilled at Tippecanoe!" ("What!" gasped a New Jersey Congressman, "For gallons you will spill torrents?")

Few Easterners dreamed that war was imminent. They did not understand the tremendous pressures on their president— including the fact that he wanted to be re-elected, and 1812 was an election year. According to a diary kept by an Ohio Senator, a group of "hot-headed, violent men," led by Henry Clay, actually informed Mr. Madison that "nothing less than open and direct war with England" would assure his renomination.

Madison, exhausted by overwork, insomnia and the relentless goading of the War Hawks, easily saw war as inevitable. He felt that he had tried every conceivable alternative.

The British were still stubbornly retaining their Orders-in-Council, prohibiting trade with the European continent. During the previous few months, they had seized eighteen American ships with cargoes valued at $1,500,000. War, "dreadful" though it was, "could not do us more injury than the present state of things," reasoned the Secretary of State, James Monroe. "And it would certainly be more honorable to the nation, and gratifying to the publick feelings." If Americans were to trade abroad

—and Jefferson's disastrous Embargo had shown that indeed they must—then they simply had to fight to protect their shipping.

Today the answer to that problem is clear: the Americans should have strengthened their fleet and fought defensively only, as they had done in a "half-war" with France in 1799-1800 and against the Barbary pirates in 1804. But, despite those spectacular successes, few people realized the potential of the tiny U.S. Navy. And President Madison was too dominated by the War Hawks, whose chief interest was on land.

Madison accepted total war, on land and sea. "He sees no end to the perplexities without it," explained his sympathetic wife. At least it would get the War Hawks off his back!

Unknown to America—the word could cross the ocean only by sail—eleven days before President Madison began composing his war message to Congress, Prime Minister Spencer Perceval was fatally shot in the House of Commons by a madman.

This changed everything. A groundswell movement had already been under way in England to revoke the Orders-in-Council, for the country was in great trouble. Napoleon reigned supreme on the European continent, his mighty empire extending from the Atlantic to the Adriatic—a tremendous area lost to British trade. The denial of the huge American market as well had thrown England into a deep depression. Recent harvests had failed, and the people were starving, desperate for American flour. Mills were closed for want of cotton. Rioting was extensive. Petitions were pouring into Parliament from frantic manufacturers: Please rescind the Orders-in-Council so that America's trade can be recovered! To all of these pleas, Prime Minister Perceval (described by one historian as "a mediocrity of the narrowest type") was deaf. But after his assassination, action became possible.

The new first minister, Lord Liverpool, acted swiftly. On June 16, 1812, amid great rejoicing, "Ringing of Bells, Bonfires, Roasting Sheep, and Processions," he rescinded the Orders. Merchants joyfully sped the departure of their ships for America. If only it was not too late! If war came, said the London *Times,* it would be the most unpopular war ever known. "Everyone would say that with happier talents it might have been avoided."

Alas, it was too late! While the British were forming a new government, President Madison was sending his war message to Congress. It carefully reviewed all the grievances against England: (1) impressment; (2) the hovering of British warships around American shores; (3) the Orders-in-Council, under which "our commerce has been plundered in every sea"; and (4) Indian warfare, which Madison found difficult to believe was not British-connected. Congress would have to decide whether the United States should "continue passive under these accumulating wrongs."

Congress received this grave message in secret session on June 1, 1812. Three days later, the House passed a declaration of war. The vote—79 to 49—reflected a country divided both politically and geographically. The South and the West voted for war. The Northeast opposed it. Every single Federalist voted "no."

Next the matter went to the Senate, where debate dragged on for two weeks. Federalist Senators tried to maintain that England might soon revoke her Orders, but the War Hawks insisted that that did not matter; the main reason for war was impressment.

Vote after vote resulted in a tie. Finally, a usually absent "drunken" Senator was "very reluctantly brought up to vote," two wavering Senators fell into line and on June 17, 1812, the measure passed—19 to 13. President Madison, looking "ghastly pale," signed the war declaration the following afternoon.

Most Americans were flabbergasted. If their country had not gone to war after the *Chesapeake* or the *Little Belt* incidents, then why fight now, when there was no direct provocation at all? The *Federal Republican* wailed, "God in His mercy has deprived our rulers of their senses!"

At the very moment of its declaration, this war had actually been avoided—a remarkable achievement, considering the many difficulties and their duration. Such misunderstanding would be impossible today, with instant communication throughout the world. Nevertheless, the War of 1812 remains a classic example of a foolish move brought about by an energetic minority.

This minority was not evil, just rather naïve. They were simple, rough-hewn, uninformed men who saw war as "a duel between two nations which, when over, would probably leave them better friends than ever before."

The venture was dreadfully ill-advised. The United States was totally unprepared for war. The treasury was low, the army was small and scattered and the navy, while proud and promising, had only six frigates in fighting condition to meet hundreds of warships of the most powerful fleet the world had ever known.

The country was dangerously divided. The wealthiest section, the Northeast, refused to contribute to "Mr. Madison's War." New Englanders withheld their money and their militia, traded illegally with the enemy and even sent delegates to a convention at Hartford to discuss secession and a separate peace with England.

Those who dreamed of seizing Canada had a rude awakening. The ill-led American Army met immediate defeat at Niagara and Detroit, and then piled up a shameful record, losing nineteen out of twenty-three major battles, fighting one to a draw and winning only three—one, the Battle of New Orleans, *after* the peace treaty had been signed.

By 1814, Napoleon was conquered in Europe, and thousands of British troops were on their way to America. That black summer, 3,000 enemy soldiers marched on Washington as President Madison fled ignominiously across the Potomac River. The Federal city was put to the torch.

All that saved America was the fact that the British were tired of war and desperately wanted peace. Negotiations began in the quaint old Flemish town of Ghent. The British representatives tried to force the Americans to cede the area between the Ohio River and the Great Lakes to the Indians, but the reaction was so explosive (one of the American representatives, Henry Clay, even packed his bags to return home) that the British finally relented. A peace treaty was drawn that restored conditions just as they had been before the war.

The Treaty of Ghent, signed on Christmas Eve, 1814, settled none of the grievances that had prompted the United States to fight. As John Quincy Adams put it, America gained "nothing but peace." Impressment was not even mentioned.

It had been a strange war, allying America with a tyrant, Napoleon Bonaparte, against Europe's most enlightened nation, England—America's own "mother," from whom she had acquired her language, her customs and her democratic institutions. The war was provoked by Britain's maritime policies, but those who had suffered most—the seafaring New Englanders— were the very ones who did not want to fight. "The war was insisted upon by the south and the west," a historian has noted, "in defense of the north, which didn't want to be defended."

Where Americans expected to do well, on land, they did poorly; where they feared destruction, on sea, they did well. Indeed, the war founded a great naval tradition and gave the country its first feeling of national pride. No one could ever forget "Don't give up the ship!" or "We have met the enemy and they are ours." A national legend was created that long night in Baltimore harbor when Francis Scott Key watched the shelling of Fort McHenry and did not know, until the dawn finally broke, whether or not "our flag was still there."

The war was neither necessary nor wise. Yet it had its benefits. Americans learned, once and for all, that Canada was not theirs "for the taking." They also managed to show both themselves and others that they could not be bullied. The astonishing success of the infant U.S. Navy against stupendous odds won the respect of the world, confirming forever the independence so dearly gained some thirty years earlier. Europe never again rode roughshod over American wishes. As such, the war was an important milestone in American history.

III

The Mexican War

Thirty-one golden years of peace followed the War of 1812. The United States, respected abroad, grew and prospered at home. Seaboard factories belched smoke from dawn until dusk, while inland fields were rich with cotton, wheat, barley and corn. Westward, vast untouched lands lay waiting for the plow.

Most of those sun-drenched, sprawling, virtually uninhabited lands were owned by Mexico, but they were right in America's path. Americans didn't realize that they weren't wanted there. They sincerely believed that, as citizens of a wonderful country, they carried true blessings wherever they went. Their "missionary complex" (and their hunger for land) made them feel that it was their "manifest destiny" to spread democracy across the continent.

Before 1819 the ownership of the vast Southwest had been debatable. By right of occupation it belonged to no one, except perhaps the Indian tribes that traversed it at will. The Spaniards had explored those lands in the seventeenth century, dotting them with a long, thin string of missions, many of which were subsequently abandoned. Those that endured were oases of life in the middle of nowhere. Most of the wilderness was never touched.

The Louisiana Purchase had brought the United States to its fringes in 1803. Where did Louisiana end and New Spain begin? No one knew, and there the matter remained until 1819, when the United States, in the process of purchasing Florida from Spain, agreed to a boundary line to the Pacific Ocean on the latitude that today divides California and Oregon. In what many Americans considered "a gross diplomatic blunder," the United States thus acknowledged Spanish owner-ship of hundreds of thousands of square miles which the Mexicans neither occupied nor seemed able to use.

The first serious American penetration of Mexican territory occurred in the fertile wilderness known as Texas. Americans did not blatantly grab the land. They obtained grants, entered it legally and developed it with difficulty.

At first the Mexicans were pleased. They had long wanted to settle Texas, but their own people were lethargic and the land was too wild and remote. Now, thanks to the sturdy, hard-working Americans, Texas promised to be a boon to all of Mexico.

The Mexican Government, therefore, encouraged American settlement, offering huge land grants to all who were interested. The only requirement was that the settlers become Mexican citizens and embrace Catholicism. The Americans gladly did this, for whatever soil they owned was their country, and opportunity was always their religion.

"Texas fever" swept America. Men boarded up their shops and homes, leaving signs proclaiming "GONE TO TEXAS!" From every state of the Union, but primarily from the South, heavily loaded oxcarts rolled into the great land, spreading themselves over an enormous area. Americans soon numbered 30,000, with hundreds more arriving daily.

The Mexicans finally became alarmed. The hordes of foreigners pouring into Texas made it look like an invasion. Officials reported that they were "Mexican" and "Catholic" in name only; they were American—aggressive and independent, with their own language and customs. "Texas can't absorb these Americans," the Mexicans finally realized. *"They* will absorb Texas!"

Their alarm was increased by the fact that President Andrew Jackson was trying to buy the area, even indicating a willingness to go as high as $5 million. Jackson clearly realized that "the purchase of Texas . . . is very important to the harmony and peace of the two republics."

The impression was somehow relayed that the Mexicans might as well sell, because they were going to lose the land anyway. Horrified, they refused. "Texas" became a sore subject, one that could not be discussed objectively. The idea of holding onto it became an obsession to the Mexicans.

The stage was set for war—a war whose basic cause was the restless, aggressive westward movement of the American people, as the Mexicans vividly learned when they sent troops to seal the long border into Texas. No sooner did they plug one hole than the Americans found another. They poured across like a flood.

In a desperate attempt to get a firm grip on Texas, the Mexicans cracked down. They closed the seaports, occupied the towns and arrested leading citizens. And, as with the American Revolution, a people long used to freedom could not stand any infringement on it.

First the Americans tried peaceful petitions, declaring that they were, and always would be, loyal Mexican citizens.

But how does one petition a government that is always in flux? Ever since Mexico's successful rebellion against Spain in 1821, "governments" had risen and fallen, as one *coup d'état* followed another. "They are always in revolution, and I believe always will be," Texas leader Stephen Austin finally decided, after a discouraging trip to Mexico City and several vain attempts to buttonhole a president before he fell. "I have had much more respect for them than they deserve."

Now General Antonio López de Santa Anna, magnificent in a diamond-studded uniform and a $7,000 gold sword, gained control of the Mexican government, revoked the Constitution of 1824 and declared himself supreme dictator. He then proceeded to garrison Texas, sending enough troops to establish martial law and convince the Texans that they would rather die than endure such tyranny.

The Texans met in convention and declared themselves officially in revolt against Santa Anna, insisting that they were fighting for their rights under the 1824 Constitution. Then the American settlers flocked to the call of arms and drove all the Mexican troops from Texas, overwhelming each command in surprise attacks.

But they must have known that they could not defy a nation of seven million so easily. In Mexico City, Santa Anna was purple with rage. Shrieking, "I shall grind them into dust!"

he began to collect the large army which he planned to personally lead into Texas.

Stephen Austin hurried to Washington for help. President Jackson was extremely sympathetic, but insisted, "The U.S. Government can't interfere in what is, after all, a domestic matter."

But the American *people* couldn't sit by while their own countrymen, "bone of our bone and flesh of our flesh," were battling a military tyranny. Newspapers hit a nerve when they urged, "You who have so liberally contributed to the aid of the *Poles,* the *Greeks,* and others who have been fighting for liberty, come forward and assist your brethren!" Americans responded from the heart, pouring arms, money and supplies into Texas.

Texas also needed men. Texas commander Sam Houston begged: ". . . Come with a good rifle and one hundred rounds of ammunition, and come soon!" So Americans came—alone, in small groups or in organized battalions.

Meanwhile, Santa Anna marched north with 7,500 troops. His destination was San Antonio, considered by many to be strategically important—"the key to Texas." The defending force—a pathetically small number under Colonel James Bowie —entrenched in an abandoned old mission called the Alamo and issued urgent appeals for more men. Among those who responded were Davy Crockett, a former Tennessee Congressman, and Lieutenant-Colonel William Travis, who later assumed command. By February 23, 1836, when Santa Anna's immense advance guard was first spotted crossing the plains, the Alamo defenders numbered about 150.

The Mexican army—7,500 strong—poured into San Antonio, raised an ominous blood-red flag from the church steeple signalling *"No Mercy!"* and encircled the Alamo. The defenders refused to withdraw, determined to hold the important post until the arrival of reinforcements. They dispatched couriers with heart-rending pleas for aid but, although several groups were planning to march to their rescue, the only help that arrived in time were thirty-two stout-hearted men from Gonzales, who slipped into the mission on its seventh night of seige.

Meanwhile, Texas leaders, meeting 150 miles to the north, took a fateful vote. On March 2, 1836, amid great excitement, they formally proclaimed the independent Republic of Texas.

The new nation was baptised with blood. When it was just four days old, Santa Anna's troops stormed the Alamo and butchered all 182 defenders, savagely bayoneting the wounded. Then they piled the ghastly remains high, doused them with oil and set them afire.

In their sixty years of history, nothing stirred the American people as much as the news of this brutal massacre. Eighteen states of the Union had had men at the Alamo. Everyone mourned—not just for Travis, Bowie and Crockett, but for all the ordinary men who had fallen with them. Although the Alamo became a symbol of magnificent courage against hopeless odds, a deep hatred for the Mexicans was born there.

The Alamo was not the only example of Mexican cruelty. "In this war there are no prisoners," Santa Anna said. At Goliad, his troops overwhelmed Colonel James Fannin and his 400 men. After imprisoning them for a week, the Mexicans brutally massacred them and then—as at the Alamo—burned their bodies.

"I shall destroy every American settlement in Texas!" Santa Anna now boasted, and his army fanned out to cut a wide

swath of death and destruction. Terrified settlers fled for
Louisiana—in carts or on foot, driving their livestock before
them.

Stephen Austin again begged President Jackson for help, so
that "the butcheries in Texas will cease, humanity will no
longer be outraged." He tried to maintain that "this is a war
of Mexicans against Americans."

But Jackson could not forget that the "Texians" were
Mexican citizens. He scolded them for declaring their independence—a step that "has aroused and united all Mexicans
against them." They should have "pondered well, it was
a rash and premature act, our neutrality must be faithfully
maintained." The United States could do nothing. Texas would
have to save herself.

The Texans' only hope lay in the fact that Santa Anna
divided his force in order to cover as much territory as possible. He raced ahead to trap Sam Houston's little army—all
that lay between him and the complete conquest of Texas.

Houston, a wily Indian fighter, skillfully maneuvered Santa
Anna into a cul-de-sac formed by the swollen San Jacinto
River and two flooded bayous. He destroyed Vince's Bridge,
the only exit from the rain-soaked area, and then he struck.

His 783 fighting-mad men burst into the Mexican camp
shrieking, "Remember the Alamo! Remember Goliad!" The
1,500 Mexicans, aroused from their siestas, tried to fight back,
but they didn't stand a chance against such righteous rage. In
just eighteen bloody minutes, the Texans killed or captured
the entire force, with only six of their own men killed and
twenty-four wounded.

Among the escaped Mexicans who were rounded up the
next day—trapped by the flooded marshes and the swift river—

was a terrified man found hiding by the splintered wreckage of Vince's Bridge. When he was brought back to camp, the other prisoners jumped to excited attention, crying, *"El Presidente!"* The trembling soldier was none other than General Santa Anna!

The Texans went wild. Many wanted to lynch him on the spot; but Houston knew that Santa Anna was most valuable alive.

When Santa Anna realized that a noose around his neck was his only alternative, he obligingly ordered all of his troops from Texas—all the scattered, unconquered commands, the thousands upon thousands of soldiers—back across the Rio Grande forever. Then, as supreme dictator of Mexico, he signed a treaty recognizing the independent Republic of Texas with its southern boundary at the Rio Grande.

Thus, in one of the most incredible stories in American history, did Texas win her independence. But Texans did not want complete independence. They wanted to join the American union, and here the incensed Mexicans drew the line. As far as they were concerned, Texas was still theirs. If the United States annexed that territory, it could mean only one thing: war. War between the United States and Mexico.

An interesting turn of events followed the independence of Texas. Americans who had enthusiastically supported the Texas Revolution suddenly realized, with horror, that Texas was slave territory. They began to think that the Revolution might have been a "slave-owners' conspiracy" to add another slave state to the Union (or maybe even four or five, considering the size of the area). Northerners vehemently opposed the admission of Texas, declaring that it would be "a blatant land grab from Mexico"; Southerners angrily demanded it. "Texas" quickly became a hornet's nest which politicians avoided.

For nine years Texans pressed in vain for statehood, at the same time desperately protecting their independence against an irate Mexico. This meant continuing guerrilla-style border warfare, with incidents that constantly refueled the hatred now raging between the two countries. Hideous Mexican atrocities reaffirmed the impression of cruelty born at the Alamo, while the Mexicans received continual confirmation that Americans were rapacious, land-hungry people eager to bite off huge sections of their country.

Americans were even then eying California—a wonderland of eternal spring, lush with gigantic forests, mineral-rich mountains and fertile valleys. They knew that the area was thinly populated—mostly by aristocratic Spaniards and their dispirited Indian slaves. It was virtually independent of faraway Mexico City, but was torn by violence and anarchy as local groups vied for power.

Americans were already beginning to move in. Many Yankee shippers, rounding the Horn, had settled there to trade in hides and tallow. Droves of covered-wagon pioneers, part of the "Great Migration" to Oregon, were turning off the rugged Oregon Trail at Bear River and breaking ground near Sacramento.

Both England and France, busily extending their empires into the Pacific, were showing a lively interest in this region. Rumor spread that the Mexican Government would sell California to either country, maybe even to Russia—*anything* to keep the hated Americans from getting it.

By 1844, all of these matters were coming to a head. America and England were in a heated dispute over Oregon's boundary;

California appeared ripe for picking by *some* power; and Texas was becoming impossible to ignore any longer.

The Union then consisted of twenty-six states—thirteen slave and thirteen free, with Wisconsin, Iowa and Minnesota (all free) and Florida (slave) almost ready for statehood. Southerners were frantic to preserve their equal footing in Congress, and Texas seemed to be their only hope. Despite Mexico's clear warning that "the incorporation of Texas in the territory of the United States" would be considered "equivalent to a declaration of war against the Mexican Republic," many Southerners were threatening secession if Texas were not admitted to the Union.

By 1844, the issues of slavery and expansion had become so divisive that the Democrats had great difficulty selecting a presidential candidate. In desperation they turned to a safe unknown, the first dark horse in political history, James Knox Polk, governor of Tennessee, "the bosom friend of Old Hickory and a pure, whole-hog Democrat."

Polk's opponent, the enormously popular Henry Clay of Kentucky, seemed certain to triumph over this unknown candidate. ("*Who* is James K. Polk?" people asked throughout the campaign.) But this was Clay's third try for the presidency, and he proceeded too cautiously—the years had mellowed the fiery young War Hawk of 1812. He was now "The Great Compromiser," adept at mending fences. He indulged in soothing double-talk, while Polk came across loud and clear, promising "All of Oregon and all of Texas!" and thus, in one bold stroke, pleasing both North and South.

Incumbent President John Tyler interpreted Polk's astonishing victory as a popular mandate for the admission of Texas. He accordingly accomplished the thorny deed, narrowly pushing passage through Congress. On March 1, 1845, three days before the expiration of his term, President Tyler signed the fateful bill, inviting Texas into the Union.

"Traitor! Coward!" many Northerners raged. "This miscreant in the White House has served well his slave-owning masters," one newspaperman cried, maintaining that the.admission of Texas was "a black day for liberty in this benighted land."

But nothing could compare with the wave of indignation that swept Mexico. The Mexican minister in Washington demanded his passports and departed, bitterly denouncing the United States for "despoiling a friendly nation of a considerable part of its territory." He called the annexation of Texas "the greatest injustice recorded in the annals of modern history."

The Mexican press clamored for war—"war at once and war to the knife!" The American menace was "ever more sinister—like a hand gloved in iron clutching the throat of a frail and bloodless nation." After the "usurpation" of Texas, "no arrangement, no friendly settlement," would be possible.

When the methodical, plodding James Polk took office, two serious wars threatened the United States—one with England over the Oregon Territory, and one with Mexico over Texas. "We should stand on our rights," Polk told his alarmed countrymen, "and leave the rest to God and country."

The new president was dull and narrow—"Polk the Mediocre." But he was also honest, daring and stubborn, and he knew exactly what he wanted for his country: Oregon, California and Texas. Few presidents have pursued their goals with such singleness of purpose, or been so stunningly successful in attaining them.

Polk wasted no time in dispatching a representative, John Slidell, to Mexico to make business proposals for the land he wanted.

Polk offered Mexico nothing for Texas, which had won its own independence and had been legally admitted into the Union. But to settle the question of its southern boundary (which Santa Anna had recognized as the Rio Grande, but which the Mexicans insisted had always been the Nueces River, 120 miles to the north), the United States offered to assume the claims of American citizens in Mexico for damages done during that country's many revolutions—an internationally adjudicated $2 million.

For New Mexico (that area between Texas and California), Polk offered $5 million.

For California, "money would be no object." Polk, frantic to beat the British to that prize, suggested $40 million.

A whopping $47 million for outer lands hardly owned by right of settlement could have been a boon to a nation that was eternally bankrupt. But emotion had already taken over. The Mexicans' intense hatred made any deal impossible. They would not even receive Slidell, much less entertain his proposals. In fact, his very arrival led to the downfall of yet another "government."

When Polk learned that Slidell had been spurned and that "a new administration of some kind or other at this moment controls that unfortunate country," he decided that only "strong measures" could push Mexico to the bargaining table.

He ordered General Zachary Taylor to take up a position on the Rio Grande with a detachment of 3,500 troops. Theoretically, this made good defensive sense, since rumors were rife that the infuriated Mexicans were about to invade Texas.

But on the *Rio Grande*—120 miles into the hotly disputed border territory? A more provocative move could hardly be imagined.

General Taylor, "Old Rough and Ready," dutifully entrenched on the swift muddy river opposite the lovely old Mexican town of Matamoros—"a most unholy and unrighteous proceeding," in the opinion of one of his officers, who wrote home: "My heart is not in this business. It looks as if the government sent a small force on purpose to bring on a war, so as to have a pretext for taking California and as much of this country as possible."

The Mexicans reacted with an ultimatum: Retire to the Nueces River within twenty-four hours or . . . *war*.

The Mexicans actually welcomed this showdown. They were eager to take on the hated *Americanos,* whose military weakness was well known. The United States, with its traditional aversion to a standing army, had only 7,000 men under arms, while Mexico maintained a superb force of 32,000 professional soldiers, seasoned by years of revolutionary fighting. European experts believed that the Mexican army was "one of the world's finest," and that America was a weak power, "fit for nothing but to fight Indians." A war with Mexico, said the Paris *Globe,* would be "ruinous, fatal," to the United States.

The Mexican president declared that "hostilities have been begun by the United States" and dispatched enough troops to Matamoros to raise the Mexican total to 8,000—more than twice the number of Americans facing them. They had orders to "attack the army which is attacking us."

The first move was that of 1,600 Mexican lancers across the Rio Grande. Sixty-three American dragoons were sent to keep an eye on them. They never returned. Two days later, their guide staggered back with the horrifying news that they had been cornered and all sixty-three either "cut to pieces or taken prisoner."

"Hostilities may now be considered to have commenced," General Taylor grimly informed the War Department.

Even before Taylor's message reached Washington, President Polk was preparing "an historical statement of our causes of complaint against Mexico."

Cabinet members nervously suggested that he await a hostile move by Mexico, but Polk told them (according to his diary) that "in my opinion we had ample cause for war, and . . . it was impossible that we could stand in status quo, or that I could remain silent much longer."

While he was laboriously composing his war message, the adjutant-general raced up the White House steps with the dispatch from General Taylor—the news of the attack on the dragoons.

Word spread fast, throwing Washington into an uproar. Many people were astonished, for tensions over Oregon at that time were uppermost in American minds. The White House was soon packed with perspiring, "greatly excited" high officials, trying to understand what on earth had happened in Texas.

Polk promptly sent his message to Congress. With its many supporting documents, it totaled 144 pages. Boiled down to essentials, it listed four reasons for going to war:

1. Mexico's refusal to receive Slidell and hear his offers.

2. Mexico's refusal to recognize the annexation of Texas and its boundary at the Rio Grande.

3. Mexico's refusal to pay the $2 million in American claims.

4. Mexico's "hostile" act on "American" soil.

Whereas "war exists by the act of Mexico itself, I invoke the prompt action of Congress to recognize the existence of war."

Neither Polk nor Congress knew to what extent war did already exist, for plenty had happened while Taylor's message was en route to Washington. The Mexicans poured across the Rio Grande in force. Taylor maneuvered courageously and won two stunning victories against tremendous odds—one at Palo Alto, where 200 of his cavalrymen routed 2,000 Mexican horsemen, and the other at Resaca de la Palma, where the Mexican army fled in such panic that its commander left behind his dress uniform and sword.

Whether this would have made any difference is not known. Congress was reluctant to declare war. Whig opponents pointed out the obvious: that Polk had provoked the hostile act by sending Taylor's force to the Rio Grande in the first place. However, in the House, the Speaker repeatedly declared the Whigs out of order and rushed through the vote. The war measure was approved 174 to 14, with 35 abstentions—an amazingly high number. The Senate passed the bill 42-2.

"Mr. Polk has got his war!" cried Whig Senator Alexander Stephens of Georgia. "May God forgive him!"

Mr. Polk got his war, and he also got Oregon, California and Texas. For sheer nerve, the man had no equal. *After* the war had begun, he refused to relax his position on Oregon: "The only way to treat John Bull is to look him straight in the eye."

When his Secretary of State, James Buchanan, cringed at the prospect of fighting both Mexico and Great Britain at the same time, Polk, who saw everything in simple "rights" and "wrongs," was "very much astonished at the views expressed by Mr. Buchanan." He indignantly declared that he would never permit "any intermeddling of any European power on this Continent."

He meant it, and the British knew it. They didn't want a war, and they settled the issue diplomatically.

But the Mexicans wanted a war. They entered it eagerly. To their astonishment, they were trounced. In fact, they did not win a single battle. Their impressive army was almost bankrupt, rotten with corruption, ill-equipped (Mexico had no industrial plant) and led by incompetent, politically appointed officers.

American forces, although fighting in a rugged, unknown country, often against fortified positions, scored one victory after another. Not that it was so easy. The Mexicans were superb fighters, and the battles were ferocious. The land was inhospitable—much of it barren, subject to drought and rife with yellow fever. Eighty-five per cent of the American deaths were the result of disease.

The Mexicans, however, suffered the most, for the invasion of any homeland is always horrible. While the regular American soldiers appeared to have behaved properly (they were strictly disciplined), contemporary accounts reveal thousands of sickening atrocities against Mexican civilians by the rough, devil-may-care American volunteers, many of whom were impossible to control. "Their cruelty," wrote one disgusted American soldier, "was only exceeded by their insubordination."

This war of conquest has always mortified Americans, for it brutally violated their idealized self-image. The goals seemed so greedy, and the victory shamefully easy. Indeed, the war appeared villainous to many even at the time. It was popular only in Texas and the Mississippi Valley states, whence came most of its volunteers.

The Whigs vociferously opposed it. One of them, a gangling young Congressman from Illinois named Abraham Lincoln, jokingly quoted a farmer's comment on land: "I ain't greedy; I only want what jines mine." He boldly challenged Polk to prove that "the soil was our where the first blood of the war was shed."

Senator Alexander Stephens declared: "The principle of waging war against a neighboring people to compel them to sell their country is not only dishonorable, but disgraceful and infamous. What! Shall it be said that American honor aims at nothing higher than land? . . . earth—gross, vile dirt!"

The Abolitionists saw the war as a nefarious plot to extend slavery. Henry David Thoreau was so strongly against the war that he refused to pay his taxes, explaining his views in his immortal "Essay on Civil Disobedience." The Massachusetts legislature declared the war to be "insupportable by honest men," and the U.S. House of Representatives actually resolved, by a bare majority of one, that the war had been "unnecessarily and unconstitutionally begun by the President of the United States."

Obviously the war was "unnecessarily begun." But in those days war was often a small concern; Americans had hardly been nipped by its horrors. No man of courage would sacrifice important goals for its prevention, and Polk's primary goal of beating the British to California seemed to him well worth a war.

The Mexicans could have escaped the trauma by simply selling their land—land that they barely controlled and were hardly using. But, as with all wars, emotion obscured the realities. If the Mexicans could have foreseen the outcome, they might have swallowed their pride and consummated the business deal, for under the terms of the Treaty of Guadalupe Hidalgo, they received a mere $15 million for all of that land—one-third of what Polk had been trying to offer.

Embarrassing though the war was, few Americans would want to undo its tremendous gains, whereby their country became a vast domain stretching from sea to sea. More than 500,000 square miles were added to its dimensions—the area that today is New Mexico, Arizona, California, Nevada, Utah and parts of Wyoming, Colorado and Oklahoma.

Certainly Polk's resolution of the issue was decisive. And who can say that a war with Mexico would not have come in any event? Incidents were bound to continue at an ever-increasing rate. Put any hard-driving, ever-moving people beside those who are languorous and easygoing, and you know full well what is going to happen—especially when the latter own vast uninhabited lands sprawling right in the path of the former.

Like the many American wars with the Indians, this was a clash of cultures, with the goals of one people directly violating those of the other. The American movement westward seemed almost part of the natural order of things, an inevitable step in the sweeping, sometimes cruel progress of civilization.

IV

The Civil War

"Slavery they can have anywhere," Edmund Burke once declared. "It is a weed that grows in every soil.'

It certainly flourished in the southern United States, and therein lay America's great paradox: in a nation conceived in liberty and dedicated to the proposition that all men were created equal, four million human beings were held in eternal bondage.

"If there be an object truly ridiculous in nature," commented an Englishman during the American Revolution, "it is an American patriot signing resolutions of independence with the one hand, and with the other brandishing a whip over his affrighted slaves."

This paradox was the underlying cause of America's Civil War. Some historians (mostly Southern) have tried to maintain that slavery was, in fact, not a cause at all. They have mentioned "tariffs" and "states' rights" and talked of a "clash of systems" without recognizing that underneath everything lay the ghastly specter of slavery.

Civil war came because the continent could no longer endure "half slave and half free." The resolution could no longer be posponed by compromise. The North could not, in all conscience, yield an inch. And the South could not bear to make the changes required.

Of all the wars America has ever fought, none was longer in the making or more seemingly inevitable than this tragic conflict. Its seeds were sown more than a hundred years before the nation was founded, and all the brilliant personalities that trooped across the stage thereafter could not stop what poet Edwin Markham described as the "whirlwind hour" from "greatening and darkening as it hurried along."

George Washington knew that emancipation was essential, not only "on the score of human dignity" but also for the preservation of the Union. Thomas Jefferson predicted that slavery, unless abolished, would be the reef upon which the ship of state would founder. "Nothing is more certainly written in the book of fate than that these people are to be free," he declared. But neither he nor Washington, within the existing structure, could even free their own.

Before 1830 most Southerners generally admitted that "slavery is an evil and an injustice." The horrors inherent in the owning of human beings were inescapable. "I am convinced that the time will come when we shall look back and wonder how Christians could sanction slavery," wrote one planter's wife. Southerners "wish there had never been a slave brought into this country," reported a visiting New Englander, and

"would make great sacrifices to emancipate them, if it could
be safely done."

But the terrible institution, flourishing after more than 200
years, was intricately woven into every aspect of the region's
life. The South's entire economic structure was built upon its
enormous investment in slaves. The plantation system, the
whole Southern way of life, all that was known and cherished,
revolved around slavery.

How could property worth millions of dollars be suddenly
devalued to zero? And how could four million illiterate, de-
pendent people suddenly be turned loose without dreadful
chaos?

"I surely will not blame them [Southerners] for not doing
what I should not know how to do myself," admitted a com-
passionate Abraham Lincoln. Although Lincoln abhorred slavery as a "monstrous injustice . . . morally wrong," he knew
that the Southern people were "just what we would be in their
situation." "If slavery did not now exist among them," he said,
"they would not introduce it. If it did now exist among us, we
should not instantly give it up." Making a basic change, however much called for, is one of the most difficult moves known
to man.

Negro slavery had once existed in all the American colonies.
Massachusetts had been the first to approve it, in 1641, followed
by Virginia and Connecticut. Had slavery been profitable for
the Yankees, they might never have opposed it, for men's
convictions seldom stray far from their pocketbooks. But New
England's rocky soil and long, harsh winters discouraged
wholesale planting. Men learned trades or turned to the sea—
activities that did not require large labor forces.

Southerners, on the other hand, naturally embraced agriculture, for their growing season was long. This enterprise required many hands. The problem was where to get them. Free men would not work for others because they could always obtain their own land, and indentured servants were available only for a limited period. Slaves proved to be the best answer— a permanent work force, obligingly supplied by British, Dutch and Yankee traders.

The tremendous temptation to resort to slavery can be seen in the astounding number of free Negroes who also became slaveholders. Most were former slaves who had been given their freedom and some land. By 1830, more than 3,600 of them owned slaves.

Slavery created a unique way of life. Instead of towns, great plantations grew along the Southern rivers. The many whites who did not own slaves were poor, uneducated and politically apathetic. The plantation master dominated the region.

What a contrast this aristocratic society was to middle-class New England! Geographic conditions had created two very different cultures, each with its own values and its own goals. The regions clashed from the very beginning, uniting only in the face of a common enemy.

Many Southerners thought that this union was a mistake. They foresaw that the North, being more powerful, would run roughshod over their interests. As it was, the aggressive Yankees very quickly cornered the South's export-import trade, siphoning off profits by acting as shippers, bankers, insurers and middlemen. Southern planters bitterly resented this. They felt that they were still colonials; they had merely changed masters.

Yet there was always the hope that the two sections might grow together. Slavery gave signs of dying out as the soil was depleted and the disadvantages of a one-crop economy (in most cases, tobacco) began to tell. Emancipation societies flourished in all the Southern states, and efforts were made to stimulate the beginnings of manufacture.

Then came one of those simple acts which can change history. In 1793 a Connecticut visitor to Georgia, Eli Whitney, observed the cotton growing wild throughout the region and became fascinated by the limitation on its use: the product was so full of stubborn green seeds that it took a full day's labor to hand-clean just one pound of it.

Whitney loved to tinker. In less than two weeks he had devised a simple machine that could draw the raw cotton through narrow slits, quickly knocking out the seeds. With this "gin" (short for "engine"), one man could clean fifty pounds of cotton a day!

Cotton swept the deep South. Production soared from five million pounds to thirty-five million within a few years. By 1850 it exceeded one billion. The South was soon producing three-fourths of the world's cotton, feeding the mills of New England and Great Britain, accounting for two-thirds of all American exports.

Gone was all interest in freeing the slaves. Now more hands were needed to till the fields, pick the cotton and work the gins. Slavery—that dying institution—was revitalized.

As planters searched continually for new lands, the cotton kingdom galloped westward. Slave states entered the Union at a fast rate, keeping constant pace with the free ones. The count was even when Missouri (slave territory) petitioned for admission in 1818 and the slave states threatened to pull ahead.

The North roared in protest; a crisis was at hand. In Virginia, Thomas Jefferson realized with sudden horror what lay ahead for his beloved country. The thought, "like a firebell in the night, awakened and filled me with terror."

Congress worked out a compromise: offset the admission of Missouri by detaching Maine from Massachusetts and making it a separate state. And, to prevent the problem from ever arising again, draw a line westward along latitude 36° 30'. All territory north of that line would be forever free; all territory south, slave.

Many people, among them Secretary of State John Quincy Adams, realized that this Missouri Compromise was "a mere preamble—a title page to a great, tragic volume."

Sectional conflicts continued unabated. The North needed tariffs to protect its industry, whereas the South, which relied upon European commerce, could only be hurt by tariff retaliations.

When the "Tariff of Abominations" was passed by Congress in 1828, tense, granite-faced John Calhoun of South Carolina began to talk of "nullification"—the idea that a state could "nullify" any Federal law it deemed "unconstitutional." Only in this way, he maintained, could a minority protect itself from "the tyranny of the majority."

And what if the Federal Government tried to enforce the law which a state had "nullified"? "The separation of the Union would inevitably follow."

As the nullification movement gathered force, people looked toward the White House. President Andrew Jackson, born and raised in South Carolina, Tennessee planter and slaveholder, staunch states' rights man—would he throw his tremendous prestige in support of the South?

"Old Hickory" smoked his pipe and said nothing. Tension mounted as the Democrats' annual Jefferson Day Dinner neared, for then Jackson would almost surely speak. Indeed, at that gala political event in the Indian Queen Hotel, the time had obviously come, for the interminable customary toasts, one after another, were to states' rights and nullification. An attempt was being made to officially commit the Democratic Party.

Finally it was the President's turn to speak. He rose to his full height and waited patiently for the cheers to subside. Then he raised his glass, looked straight at John Calhoun and declared in a voice loud and clear: "Our Union: It must be preserved."

An aghast silence followed. Calhoun turned white. With shaking hands he groped for his glass, spilling the wine. "He's going to pour it out," someone whispered. But Calhoun drank. Then he lifted his glass, his eyes blazing, and offered his historic modification: "The Union: Next to our liberties, most dear."

Thus were drawn the lines of civil war.

For two years Jackson's bold stand held the nullifiers at bay. But the tariff was hurting, and near the end of 1832, South Carolina acted, officially declaring the tariff null and void and "not binding upon this State or its citizens." Any use of force to collect the duties, it warned, would be met by secession.

"No state . . . has a right to secede," rejoined Andrew Jackson. "The Union must be preserved, without blood if this be possible, but it must be preserved at all hazards and at any price."

In his great Proclamation on Nullification, Jackson declared nullification to be an "impractical absurdity": "If this doctrine had been established at an earlier day the Union would have been dissolved in its infancy." He firmly denied the right of secession: "The Constitution . . . forms a *government* not a league. . . . To say that any State may at pleasure secede from the Union is to say that the United States is not a nation."

South Carolina remained defiant. Its governor promised to maintain the sovereignty of his state or perish "beneath its ruins." South Carolinians mobilized for war.

"They are trying me here," Jackson cried, "you will witness it; but, by God in Heaven, I will uphold the laws."

Moving swiftly, he isolated South Carolina from all support. He secured through manipulation, cajolery or actual threats resolutions from all the state legislatures condemning South Carolina's action. He announced that he had "a tender of volunteers from every state in the union." He could if need be, "which God forbid," march 200,000 men "to quell any . . . insurrection."

This scrappy old man terrified people. Even Calhoun turned "pale as death" and trembled "like an aspen leaf," according to one witness, when told that Jackson had vowed to "try Calhoun for treason and, if convicted, hang him as high as Haman" if he did not cease his nullification activities. As Senator Thomas Benton had once commented, "I tell you . . . when Jackson begins to talk about hanging, they can begin to look for the ropes."

Before such formidable determination (and Jackson's promise of tariff reform), South Carolina yielded. On March 15, 1833, the proud state rescinded its nullification ordinance.

Old Hickory had nipped a rebellion in the bud by swift and bold action, but the basic problem remained, and it would grow even stickier. Jackson well knew that the real issue was slavery. "The Nullifiers . . . intend to blow up a storm on the slave question," he warned. "This ought to be met, for be assured these men would do any act to destroy this union and form a southern confederacy bounded, north, by the Potomac River."

The problem was already being complicated by the fact that

slavery was becoming a moral issue. This could have been an excellent development had the nation united in accepting responsibility, but, unfortunately, it took the form of Northerners sitting in judgment upon the South.

In 1831 a young Boston printer, William Lloyd Garrison, issued a shocking periodical, *The Liberator,* in which he angrily attacked the "conspiracy of silence" protecting slavery in the United States. "I am in earnest—I will not equivocate—I will not excuse—I will not retreat a single inch—AND I WILL BE HEARD." Garrison boldly expressed what most Americans, even Southerners, knew in their hearts to be true: that slavery was wrong. But Garrison's angry cry of "sinner!" touched an open nerve. Southerners, already tortured from within by their own consciences, could not bear this additional criticism from outside.

They were horrified as a growing number of Northerners began to demand immediate abolition of slavery, flooding the South with "freedom" broadsides which urged the blacks to "throw off the yoke and wash away in blood" the sins of their masters.

The birth of this Abolitionist movement was followed by a terrifying event in Southampton County, Virginia: In August, 1831, a "divinely" inspired Negro named Nat Turner led some seventy fellow slaves on a wild rampage, killing fifty-seven whites, including women and children. Although this rebellion was swifty crushed, the South was never the same again.

A slave insurrection had long been the South's most dreaded nightmare. The wealthy whites, isolated on their remote plantations, were overwhelmingly outnumbered by the blacks who tilled their fields. Now they lived in constant terror. "It is like a smothered volcano," wrote one Virginia lady. "We know not when, or where, the flame will burst forth, but we know that death in the most repulsive form awaits us."

In their fear Southerners began to see Abolitionist conspiracies everywhere. They formed vigilante committees, censored the mail, burned books, withdrew their sons from Northern colleges and even jailed native-born Southerners for "inflammatory" ideas. Although most Southerners did not even own slaves, all closed ranks on this matter. No one wanted the blacks incited to rebellion; it was a matter of public safety.

Thus at a time when the nation, North and South, should have been working together to eradicate slavery, Southerners were tightening its bonds. To ease their guilt, they concocted elaborate rationalizations, insisting that their "ancestral institution" was not an evil but a *positive good*. They quoted the Bible; they quoted Aristotle, who thought slavery was "necessary." They convinced themselves that Negroes were subhuman beings, divinely created to be "hewers of wood and drawers of water."

"Many in the South once believed that slavery was a moral and political evil," declared Calhoun. "That folly and delusion are gone. We see it now in its true light, and regard it as the most sane and stable basis for free institutions in the world."

If any Northerners were swayed by these arguments, they were dramatically re-educated in 1852 by a woman who earnestly wanted to "make the whole nation feel what an accursed thing slavery is." Harriet Beecher Stowe's melodramatic novel, *Uncle Tom's Cabin,* burst upon the American scene with an impact as enormous as that of Thomas Paine's *Common Sense.* It was a shocker—so graphically depicting the horrors of slavery that millions of apathetic Northerners were quickly aroused. Southerners, on the other hand, bitterly resented Mrs.

Stowe's highly imaginative portrayal. After the publication of *Uncle Tom's Cabin,* passion took over. North and South could no longer communicate.

Some historians have criticized Mrs. Stowe and her fellow Abolitionists for so hopelessly polarizing the nation. Certainly their "holier than thou" approach would have antagonized anyone, and their hatred was destructive. Many Abolitionists frankly wanted war—"a terrible remedy for a terrible wrong." Most welcomed disunion. Nathaniel Hawthorne "rejoiced" when Southern states began seceding: "We never were one people, and never really had a country since the Constitution was formed."

Few Northerners shared these extreme views, agreeing with the old woman who grunted, "Of all things in the world, I hate slavery the most—except abolitionism."

Still, human nature being what it is, someone was bound to point an accusing finger at the slaveholding South. The Abolitionists saw only the moral issue and had no concern for the practical problems, but the South was equally remiss: it was so overwhelmed by the practical problems that it became blind to the moral issues.

In the 1850s, no Southern leader emerged to help the people face the painful truth. One and all encouraged the prevailing delusions. So the South clung to its inefficient and outmoded system while the rest of the country raced toward the twentieth century.

The North was progressing rapidly, industrializing at a whirling pace, leaving the feudalistic South far behind. America was soon "a continent of almost distinct nations," according to a European visitor, who "never failed to mark the difference on entering a slave state." The South was trying to stand still, and, therefore, was doomed. For when the old and the new clash, the new sooner or later triumphs.

The South could only hope to delay the inevitable. The North had already pulled ahead in population, and one look at the map revealed vast new territory that was destined to enter the Union as free states. Southerners would soon be at the political mercy of a people who hated them. "The South, oh the poor South" cried John Calhoun. "What will become of her?"

Although dying, Calhoun dragged himself into the Senate chamber to plead for a Constitutional amendment "to restore to the South the power she possessed . . . before the equilibrium between the two sections was destroyed." Failing this, he warned, the South would have to "part in peace" because she simply could not, "in keeping with honor and safety," remain in the Union.

Terrified of civil war, many people tried to placate the South. The two aged patriots, Daniel Webster and Henry Clay, even offered, in their Compromise of 1850, a stronger fugitive slave law in return for the admission of California as a free state. Webster and Clay could not see that their compromises were mere bandages over deep wounds. Underneath, the sores continued to fester.

The new fugitive slave law nourished the very germ that was causing the illness. The North just could not accept it. "I will not obey it, by God!" cried Ralph Waldo Emerson. As runaway slaves were hunted down in Northern streets and returned under arms to the South, Northern feeling rose dangerously. Indignant crowds rescued Negroes from courtrooms or attempted to break open their jail cells.

With the country in such turmoil, almost anything could

have triggered the deadly cycling that leads to war. The deed
was the Kansas-Nebraska Act of 1854, which gave birth to a
new, totally sectional political party (the Republican) and
split the Democrats hopelessly in two—permitting the triumph
of the Republicans in 1860. The triumph of the Republicans,
in turn, provoked the secession of the Southern states, which
in turn provoked the war.

The Kansas-Nebraska Act, passed after tremendous controversy and an uproar which resounded throughout the
North, reopened the entire West to slavery, erasing the sacred
assurance of the Missouri Compromise that all territory north
of latitude 36° 30′ would be "forever free." America's un-
settled prairies were thrown open to everyone, with "popular
sovereignty"—the wishes of the settlers—eventually deciding
whether the land was to be free or slave.

Now a wild scramble began between slave and anti-slave
forces for possession of the Kansas-Nebraska area. "We are
playing for a mighty stake," cried Missouri's pro-slavery Senator, D. R. Atchison. "If we win, we carry slavery to the Pacific
Ocean."

Northerners determinedly poured into Kansas, "an Abolitionist invasion," in the view of pro-slavery Missourians, who invaded the area in gangs to stop them, "armed to the teeth with
Revolvers, Bowie Knives, Rifles, & Cannon." After a Missouri
army sacked the free-soil town of Lawrence, an outraged
Abolitionist settler, John Brown, conducted a grisly midnight
raid of scattered cabins, pulling innocent farmers and their
teen-age sons from their beds and, despite the pleas of their
wives and mothers, hacking them to death with heavy sabers.
This triggered more retaliation, and soon guerrilla bands on
both sides were attacking settlements, burning houses and con-

ducting a general reign of terror. The nation was graphically shown that free and slave men could not live together peacefully.

Northerners, already raging mad over numerous slave incidents and the passage of the Kansas-Nebraska Act, became almost uncontrollable when they learned that thousands of Missourians had crossed the border to vote illegally for slavery, fighting their way into the Kansas polls and stuffing the ballot boxes. They were especially enraged when they learned that James Buchanan, the Democratic President, supported the results.

Incidents now came fast and furious. In the Senate, a South Carolina Congressman beat Abolitionist Charles Sumner senseless at his desk, pounding his head repeatedly with a heavy guttapercha cane until the cane actually broke, and then continuing the assault with the splintered stump. Sumner remained an invalid for the rest of his life.

The Southern-dominated Supreme Court handed down a decision in the case of Dred Scott, ruling that a Negro born of a slave, even if he appeared to have been freed, was "an article of merchandise," could not be a citizen, had no rights and could sue no one. Furthermore, the Court ruled that Congress could not forbid slavery in the territories.

This was too much for a people who had come to view slavery as a moral issue. The North felt that if a decision like Dred Scott could be handed down, then something was terribly wrong with the country.

Distressed almost beyond endurance, many turned to the new Republican Party, born in direct opposition to the Kansas-Nebraska Act. Here they found the answers they had long been seeking. While the Democrats prattled nervously about

appeasing the South, the Republicans made their position remarkably clear: they would keep their hands off slavery where
it already existed (in the hope that it would die a natural death
or that Southerners would finally abolish it themselves), but
they would halt its further spread.

Here was the gut issue that would divide the country and
lead to civil war, for on this there could be no compromise.
Either slavery expanded, or it didn't. The slaveholding South
had to expand both politically and economically in order to
survive; therefore, it was an irresistible force. Resisting it now
was an immovable object: the Republican Party, all Northerners, saying *No.*

Southerners quickly saw these Republicans as inimical to
their life interests. They became convinced that if a Republican
were elected president of the Union, they would have to secede
from that Union or die.

Their fears escalated after October, 1859, when the fanatical,
deranged John Brown invaded the sleepy Virginia mountain
hamlet of Harper's Ferry in a wild attempt to incite a massive
slave revolt. Brown, who was sick of "Talk! talk! talk! That
will never free the slaves," had determined upon "action—
action." He and his followers captured the U.S. arsenal and
took general possession of the town, killing several people in
the process.

Brown's raid was foolish and ill-conceived. No slaves
swarmed to his standard, and he and his men were easily
crushed, swiftly tried, convicted and hanged. Still, the South
had been hit where it was most vulnerable: *slave insurrection!*

Panic swept the cotton kingdom. Rumors flew. Armies of
Abolitionists were preparing to invade the South to incite the
blacks to "rapine and murder." The North was determined to
make the South "another Haiti."

In the distraught Southern mind, "John Brown," "Abolitionist," "Northerner" and "Republican" all became one and the same. When Abraham Lincoln was nominated to run for president on the Republican ticket in 1860, his name automatically joined the list. (Such errors are common before wars; many Northerners were seeing all Southerners as Simon Legrees.)

It was useless for Lincoln to point out that "John Brown was no Republican, and you have failed to implicate a single Republican in his Harper's Ferry enterprise." Lincoln could firmly denounce Brown's act, saying that nothing could "excuse violence, bloodshed and treason," but the South was not listening. Lincoln's reiterated belief that he had "no legal right" to "interfere with . . . slavery where it exists" fell upon deaf ears. Southerners were convinced—despite all of Lincoln's words to the contrary—that Lincoln, that "blackhearted abolitionist fanatic," was dedicated to the violent destruction of slavery and the Southern way of life.

Emotion, one of the basic ingredients of war, had grabbed the reins, and reality had been left far behind.

The country had started to come apart at the seams long before the election of 1860. That event merely broke the last threads.

One of the first ominous ruptures had occurred in the churches. Most of the Protestant denominations (the Methodists as early as 1842) split over the slavery issue into two separate institutions, Northern and Southern.

The political parties fell apart the same way. The Whigs broke over slavery in 1852 and crumbled into oblivion. The Democrats were critically injured by the Kansas-Nebraska Act, when Northerners left the party in droves; then, in 1860, Southern Democrats bolted to form their own organization.

The presidential ballot that year graphically dramatized the breakup of the country: each section offered its own candidate.

It was obvious from the start that the Republicans would win. The voting power lay with the North, and there the appeal of the Republican Party was tremendous, especially since the Republican candidate was the only man in the country who seemed to be making any sense. The tall, gaunt frontier lawyer, Abraham Lincoln, had become famous for his unusual ability to slice through to the nub of a problem. "All they ask we could readily grant if we thought slavery right," he explained, speaking of the Southerners. "All we ask they could as readily grant, if they thought it wrong. Their thinking it right and our thinking it wrong is the precise fact upon which depends the whole controversy."

On November 6, 1860, 4,700,000 Americans went to the polls and elected Abraham Lincoln president of the United States, giving him 180 electoral votes against a combined total of 123 for his three opponents. The voting was purely sectional: Lincoln's name was not even on the ballot in ten Southern states. But the process was nevertheless legal, and the man won honestly.

The South was horrified. "The prospect before us in regard to our Slave Property, if we continue to remain in the Union is nothing less than utter ruin," one planter wrote in his diary. The people felt that they had no choice but to secede.

On December 20, 1860, a South Carolina convention unanimously resolved, to deafening cheers, the pealing of church bells and the booming of guns, that "the Union now subsisting between South Carolina and other states, under the name of the United States of America, is hereby dissolved."

Six other states rapidly left the Union—Mississippi, Florida,

Alabama, Georgia, Louisiana and Texas. With South Carolina, they formed a new slaveholding republic: the Confederate States of America.

The lame-duck president, James Buchanan, was appalled. Tears streamed down his cheeks as he foresaw "bloody, fraticidal war," but he took no action.

The president-elect, Abraham Lincoln, probably would have. "If you attempt it [secession]," he had previously told the South, *"we won't let you.* With the purse and the sword, the army and navy and treasury in our hands . . . you couldn't do it."

"We have dissolved the Union!" now cried Texan Louis Wigfall. "Mend it if you can; cement it with blood; try the experiment."

Senator Jefferson Davis of Mississippi pleaded with the North to let the Southern states depart in peace, "since we cannot live peaceably together." He insisted, "All we ask is to be let alone."

Was secession, after all, really such a sin? Had not the American colonies "seceded" from Great Britain? Was it not a sacred American principle that a people, in defense of their rights, could declare their independence and form their own government?

Lincoln thought not. He saw secession as a first step to a continent of many countries, torn like Europe, with wars over boundary lines and fugitive slaves. The principle of "secession" directly challenged the sacred concept of "Union," and to most Northerners this became the urgent issue, with slavery taking a back seat. The very stability of the government was now at stake.

Lincoln made it clear that he deemed secession to be illegal. As far as he was concerned, "the Union is unbroken; and to the extent of my ability, I shall take care . . . that the laws of the Union shall be faithfully executed in all the States." Whatever happened, "the power confided to me will be used to hold, occupy and possess the property and places belonging to the government."

Never has a new American president been faced with such critical problems. The South had demanded the evacuation of Federal troops from the man-made rock island of Fort Sumter in Charleston harbor. When Lincoln took office, that fort was already surrounded by powerful shore batteries and its small garrison cut off from all supplies. A decision had to be made immediately: the fort's food supply would run out about the middle of April; should Lincoln try to reprovision it?

"Let your President attempt to reinforce Sumter," warned the governor of South Carolina, "and the tocsin of war will be sounded from every hilltop and valley in the South."

When fearful Northerners urged Lincoln to avert war by surrendering the Federal fort, Lincoln retorted bitterly, "I would like to know from you what I am to do with my oath of office." He notified Southern authorities that he was dispatching food supplies to Fort Sumter.

After receiving this information, Confederate leaders discussed attacking the fort. Secretary of State Robert Toombs warned, "The firing on that fort will inaugurate a civil war greater than any the world has yet seen. You will wantonly strike a hornet's nest which extends from mountains to ocean; legions, now quiet, will swarm out and sting us to death."

But Confederate president Jefferson Davis felt that as long as Federal troops remained in South Carolina, the secession of that state was a farce. He sent the fort one last ultimatum.

"I do not pretend to sleep," a Charleston woman wrote in her diary during the early hours of April 12, 1861. "How can

I? If Anderson [commander of Fort Sumter] does not accept terms at four, the orders are he shall be fired upon. I count four, St. Michaels' bells chime out and I begin to hope. . . ."

At half-past four a flash on shore "as of distant lightning, followed by the dull roar of a mortar," launched a shell high among the stars, its flaming fuse sputtering in the dark before it exploded over Fort Sumter. Within seconds all the encircling shore batteries opened fire, beginning a bombardment which persisted all that day, that night and throughout the next, pounding the fort with more than 3,000 shot and shell.

The defenders fired back until they were forced to retire within their casements. Then they hugged the ground with wet handkerchiefs over their mouths and eyes to keep out the smoke. Their situation was hopeless. They finally ran up a white flag, and at twelve noon, Sunday, April 14, 1861, the Palmetto flag of South Carolina was raised over the installation.

As Secretary Toombs had predicted, the firing on the American flag struck a hornet's nest from mountains to ocean, arousing a whirlwind of Northern patriotism.

President Lincoln grimly proclaimed the seven Confederate states has having "combinations too powerful to be suppressed" by ordinary procedures and called upon "the militia of the several States of the Union, to the aggregate number of 75,000," to "suppress said combinations, and to cause the laws to be duly executed." Men rushed to volunteer their services.

In the border states, however, many people realized with horror that they could not fight their own kin. Lincoln's call for troops triggered the secession of North Carolina, Tennessee, Arkansas and the great, prestigious state of Virginia, which only eight days before Fort Sumter had rejected secession by a two-to-one vote. Knowing that Federal troops would have to cross Virginia to "make war on the South," the governor of that state called upon his people to defend their land as they had against the British. The Virginia legislature, some of its members weeping openly, voted to leave the Union which its most revered heroes had worked with all their resources to build.

The secession of those four states increased the population of the Southern Confederacy by some 8o per cent, brought it valuable minerals and industries, extended its borders to the very shores of the federal capital and placed at its disposal some of the best military talent of the war.

After this calamity, Lincoln moved swiftly, even ruthlessly, to hold the teetering states of Missouri, Kentucky and Maryland. He succeeded, and the battle lines were drawn.

With one section of the country pitted squarely against the other, the war became—like most wars—geographical. Only where the two regions met did there exist, to any degree, the characteristics of true civil war: consciences torn, with brother fighting against brother. People elsewhere automatically supported their own area. The issues that had caused the war ceased to matter. Like Robert E. Lee, who did not believe in secession and thought that slavery was "a moral and political evil," few men could bring themselves to "raise my hand against my relatives, my children, my home."

Gone were all the old rationalizations about slavery being a "positive good." Not one of the great Virginia generals owned slaves (whereas the Union general, Ulysses S. Grant, owned two throughout much of the war—they belonged to his wife, the daughter of a Missouri planter). Human consciences were already reawakening. Indeed, when the Confederacy was on its last legs, the nation was willing, even eager, to liberate its slaves, if by so doing it could save its life. And as the years passed, Southerners would become more and more vehement in their insistence that the war had never been fought over slavery.

Southerners fought for independence, self-government and —in the face of invasion—self-defense. In this, their "Second War for Independence," they drew their inspiration from America's first; throughout the ordeal, General Lee was sustained by the example of his great idol, George Washington.

Southerners were *certain* that their cause was just—they were fighting, after all, to defend the only life they knew. "If General Lee has had to surrender then there is no God in heaven!" cried a heartbroken soldier at Appomattox. "They say *right* always triumphs, but what cause could have been more just than ours?" confided a weeping woman to her diary. "I *cannot* understand it. I never loved my country as I do now. I feel I could sacrifice *everything* to it."

"Each party claims to act in accordance with the will of God," observed President Lincoln. "Both read the same Bible, and pray to the same God; and each invokes His aid against the other."

Southerners fought as only men can fight who *know* that they are right. What they lacked in numbers and industry, they made up for in spirit and tenacity. "We can call out a million of people, if need be," declared Confederate vice-president Alexander Stephens, "and when they are cut down, we can call out another, and still another, until the last man of the South finds a bloody grave."

A British military observer became convinced "that the South can only be forced back by such a conquest as that which laid Poland prostrate at the feet of Russia." General Sherman predicted, "The country will be drenched in blood."

He was right. The war was a national disaster. The casual-

ties staggered the imagination. More Americans died in the
Civil War than in all other American wars combined—over
600,000—and at a time when the country's population was
one-seventh of what it is today. The losses, in terms of population, were greater than those of any war in modern history.

In *one day,* at Antietam, more than twice as many Americans were killed than in the *entire* War of 1812, while the
Gettysburg deaths far exceeded all American battle deaths
in the War of 1812, the Mexican War and the Spanish-American War *combined.* Truly all America, North and South,
could gasp, along with the horrified officer at Fredericksburg,
"Oh, great God! See how our men, our poor fellows, are
falling!"

Among the grimmest statistics were prisoner deaths: 61,308
Northerners and Southerners—more than were killed in battle
in either World War I *or* the Korean War *or* Vietnam. "In
the name of all that is holy," a South Carolina woman wrote
her governor concerning a nearby prison camp, "is there
nothing that can be done to relieve such dreadful suffering?"

Probably no one felt these losses as acutely as the man in
the White House, who was often "as inconsolable as I can be
and still live." After Antietam, a visitor found Lincoln "literally bending under the weight of his burdens. A deeper gloom
rested on his face than on that of any other person I had ever
seen." When told that Fredericksburg "was not a battle, it
was a butchery," Lincoln was "heartbroken . . . and soon
reached a state of nervous excitement bordering on insanity."
When rebuked for telling jokes in times of such grief, he
cried, "Don't you see that if I didn't laugh I would have to
weep?" To a man who had lost a son at Gettysburg, Lincoln
confided, "My heart is like lead within me, and I feel like

hiding in deep darkness." When he learned that Grant had lost some 54,000 in the Wilderness campaign—more than half the number of Lee's entire force—he dropped his head into his hands and groaned, "My God! My God! My God!"

Yet he never faltered in his conviction that the Union must be preserved, in the words of Andrew Jackson, "at all hazards and at any price." Future generations *must* be shown that "there can be no successful appeal from the ballot to the bullet."

When fainter hearts pleaded for an armistice, for compromise terms with the South, for anything to stop the dreadful bloodletting, Lincoln insisted firmly, "There is no alternative but to keep pegging away."

With supreme patience, wisdom and political skill, he kept his people behind him, and they responded with patriotism and love: "We are coming, Father Abraham, three hundred thousand more."

Against his leadership and resolution, the South was lost.

Lincoln's assassination less than one week after the war ended was the greatest single tragedy in American history.

For the South it was a calamity. Lincoln was one of the few people in those bitter days who did not succumb to hatred. "How can you speak kindly of our enemies," an irate woman once asked him, "when you should instead destroy them?"

"What, madam?" replied Lincoln. "Do I not destroy them when I make them my friends?"

Visiting the Confederate wounded, Lincoln told them that he bore them no malice; they had become foes through "uncontrollable circumstances."

His advice, as the war drew to an end and people talked of

"hanging the rebel leaders," was simple: "I'd let 'em up easy."

He wanted only to reunite the bleeding nation, exhibiting "malice toward none, charity for all," and achieve, hopefully, "a just and lasting peace."

Once he was dead, however, all the forces of hatred, so skillfully kept in tow, were unleashed, and the vanquished, as though they had not suffered enough, were denied the aid they so desperately needed.

The South was in ruins, its economy smashed, its manhood decimated, the survivors maimed and ailing. "Mourning in every household," wrote General Sherman, "cities in ashes and fields laid waste, their commerce gone, their system of labor annihilated. . . . Ruin, poverty and distress everywhere, and now pestilence adding the very capsheaf to their stack of miseries."

There was no shelter, no money, no seed, no stock, no tools. Fighting sheer starvation, many Southerners could not even educate their children. They would be mired in poverty for almost a hundred years, the "problem" region of the nation, highest in illiteracy and disease, trailing in every area of progress and reform.

The plight of the Negroes was worst of all. When they were freed, few were ready to fend for themselves; not one in a thousand could read or write. Struggling for existence amid the wreckage of the land, many continued their old master-slave relationships, preserving the essence of slavery without the benefits of total care. The lawlessness attending their mass emancipation led to a reaction among the whites that encased them for a hundred years in a caste system as rigid as the one in India.

President Lincoln, forseeing these dangers of abrupt liberation, had devised a superb plan for the gradual, compensated emancipation of all slaves, which he presented in December, 1861. It is worth studying in detail, for it is a blueprint on how the Civil War might have been avoided, had it only been formulated in time and accepted by the American people.

Other countries managed to abolish slavery without the major surgery of civil war, but America was cursed with a particularly sticky complication: a *sectional* concentration of her slavery, with all the attending problems of sectional interests and pride. The only hope of avoiding war—and this had to occur before passions became too heated—was for the North to recognize slavery as a *national* problem and not condemn it as a Southern sin, and for the South to face reality and prepare for emancipation.

The clue to the war's inevitability lay in the psychology of the Abolitionists and the corresponding psychology of a very defensive, fearful South. Once those complex emotions were brought into play, there was no hope of a peaceable solution. The march of events—most particularly the industrialization and expansion of the nation—with their inherent threat to the South, was obviously inexorable. The accounting had to come —a horrendous collision of two systems in which one was completely destroyed.

It is not true, as some people say, that war never accomplishes anything. This war abolished slavery—at least formally —and, above all, it reaffirmed the basic Federal principle regarding secession. Today it is clearly understood that no state can secede. The world has been dramatically shown that "this nation or any nation so conceived . . . can long endure." Whatever else happened, the American "government of the people, by the people, for the people" did not perish from the earth.

V

The Spanish-American War

Americans were still recovering from the devastating Civil War when momentous events began to occur on the Spanish-owned island of Cuba, ninety miles off the tip of Florida. In 1868, some one hundred excited Cuban planters raised the cry of *"Independencia!"* and started a revolution against Spain.

Americans could not ignore this event so close to home. They naturally sympathized with any people rebelling against a colonial power. And there were incidents that affected Americans. American adventurers engaged in gun smuggling had some of their ships seized by the Spaniards. The crew of one was actually marched out in platoons and shot.

The Cuban revolution ended after ten years when the Spaniards persuaded the exhausted rebels to lay down their arms, promising them amnesty and reform but not independence. Many of the rebels emigrated to the United States, where they continued to dream of *"Cuba libre,"* keeping alive the old passions with oratory and demonstrations.

By early 1895, they were ready to strike again. They arranged for simultaneous uprisings throughout the island to coincide with their own landings. This second revolution was well planned, and the insurgents were remarkably successful.

They knew that they could not defeat the Spaniards on the battlefield, so they pursued a guerrilla war. Their strategy was one of devastation and terror, aimed at destroying the entire economy. They burned the cane fields, shot any laborers reporting for work, ravaged crops, wrecked railroads and beseiged the towns, cutting the inhabitants off from all food supplies.

By January, 1896, the rebels had spread havoc across the entire island, leaving famine in their wake. At night the glow of burning cane fields could be seen from Havana.

The desperate Spanish Government sent General Valeriano Weyler to crush the rebellion and restore order. Weyler found the island in a deplorable state. He declared martial law and garrisoned the country, "reconcentrating" the peasants into fortified areas where they could not help the rebels.

He successfully isolated the rebel forces, rendering them almost powerless. They were now "always hungry," according to an American fighting with them. Their "pack trains scoured the country, taking from the miserable people the last sweet potato, ear of corn or banana that could be found."

Their only hope now lay with America. Recognizing that "without a press, we shall get nowhere," they pursued a strenuous propaganda campaign, feeding American reporters horrible stories of Spanish atrocities and stressing the suffering of the Cuban people, which they themselves had provoked but which they now blamed on Weyler's reconcentration policy.

Americans fell for this propaganda, sincerely believing that Weyler was a "butcher." They gasped at the headlines splashed across their newspapers: "SPANIARDS MURDER HUNDREDS OF HELPLESS STARVING CUBANS!" "WEYLER WAGES WAR NOT ON MEN BUT ON WOMEN!"

They did not realize that their newspapers were printing anything that might boost circulation. Reader competition in those days was intense. In New York, William Hearst of the *Journal* and Joseph Pulitzer of the *World* were waging a fantastic circulation war, each determined to outsell the other. Both shamelessly magnified every incident of the rebellion, sending hordes of reporters south in search of juicier tidbits.

Under such circumstances, there was little concern for the truth. Americans recently returned from Cuba, where Weyler had established a relative calm, were astonished to read of the "desperate fighting" raging on that island. They concluded that "the rebellion was being fought mostly in the newspapers."

When illustrator Frederic Remington wired Hearst, "Everything is quiet. There is no trouble. There will be no war. I wish to return," Hearst issued his famous reply: "Please remain. You furnish the pictures and I'll furnish the war."

The *Journal* printed heartbreaking descriptions of the suffering *reconcentrados*. "They fall dead in the streets; they die before your eyes . . . in the wretched pens where they are huddled together." The *World* described whole villages of "living skeletons praying for death to release them."

Never have newspapers laid it on so thick. The accounts of Spanish atrocities were endless: "I found the place where the victims had been hurriedly buried. A few strokes of a spade uncovered the ghastly evidences of murder. The hands of the slain Cubans were tied behind their backs. The sight revealed . . . would have moved the hardest heart."

Americans were horrified. How could they stand idly by while such crimes were being committed on their very doorstep? Newspapers demanded war: "Intervention has become a duty!"

But President Grover Cleveland thought that "it would be an outrage to declare war." He criticized the press for "arousing sentimental sympathy" for the rebels. Staunchly refusing to bow to public pressure, he declared, "There will be no war with Spain over Cuba while I am president."

His successor, the kindly William McKinley, tried to follow his example. "If I can only go out of office at the end of my term with . . . the success [in staying out of war] that has crowned your patience and persistence," he told Cleveland on the eve of his inauguration, "I shall be the happiest man in the world."

But the country was ripe for another war. More than thirty years had passed since the end of the Civil War, and some of its horrors had faded. The United States was settled from coast to coast—the census director had announced the closing of the frontier in 1890—and the Indians, after three centuries of bloody conflict, were finally, forever vanquished. The bustling Americans needed new outlets for their energies. As the *Overland Review* so bluntly put it, "Now that the continent is subdued, we are looking for fresh worlds to conquer."

The United States had become a great industrial power—the world's largest coal, wheat, machinery, iron and steel producer. Its factories were making more goods and its farms producing more crops than its own people could possibly consume. New markets were needed.

Americans were proud of their strength, eager to take their rightful place on the world stage and hypersensitive to any hint that their country was not a major power. The people were furious when *American* correspondents in Cuba were imprisoned by the Spaniards (one was tied to a tree and hacked to death), when *American* ships were stopped on the high seas and searched for contraband and when the *American* president was described by the Spanish Ambassador as "weak and a bidder for the admiration of the crowd . . . a common politician." They believed that America was tolerating "what no European power would have tolerated."

Many Congressmen were ambitious for their country. Observing the major nations rapidly acquiring colonies, Senator Henry Cabot Lodge thought that the United States should not "fall out of the line of march." He declared, "We have a record of conquest, colonization and expansion unequaled by any people in the nineteenth century. We are not to be curbed now."

"It is time that someone woke up and realized the necessity of annexing some property," insisted another Congressman. "We want all this northern hemisphere."

"We certainly ought to have that island [Cuba]," agreed Senator William Frye. "And if we cannot buy it, I for one would like to have an opportunity to acquire it by conquest."

It began to sound like 1812, but instead of "Canada! Canada! Canada!" Congressmen were crying "Cuba! Cuba! Cuba!" They were encouraged by the fact that the Spaniards had long passed their prime. "They are beaten, broken and out of the race and are proud and know it," Senator Lodge reported after a visit to Madrid. Weakness always invites aggression.

Ardent imperialists like Assistant Secretary of the Navy Theodore Roosevelt did not overlook the fact that Spain had Pacific, as well as Atlantic, possessions. Roosevelt thought the U.S. Navy should "blockade, and, if possible, take Manila." He pulled strings to appoint an aggressive commander, George Dewey, to the Asiatic Squadron, and then, taking advantage of the temporary absence of his superior, Secretary of the Navy John Long, one historic afternoon, he "in his precipitate way" (the words are Long's), put into motion all the necessary wheels. Roosevelt, as though "possessed by the very devil," redistributed ships, ordered enormous amounts of ammunition and cabled Dewey in Hong Kong to "keep full of coal" and, "in the event of declaration of war with Spain," begin "offensive operations in the Philippine Islands."

For those who were squeamish, this aggressiveness could always be rationalized under the old "missionary complex." Americans had long believed that it was their "manifest destiny" to spread their blessings across the continent. Now that the continent was settled, it was a simple matter to extend that concept to other, more distant regions.

"The Cubans look upon the [American] flag today as the emblem of liberty, as we look upon the cross as the emblem of Christianity," declared one Congressman. "And wherever you would advance the cross . . . I would take that flag."

It is little wonder that Congressmen, driven by such emotions, accepted the misinformation served by the "yellow" press. Senator William Allen thought it "conclusively established that Spanish soldiers had . . . taken little infants by the heels, held them up and hacked them to pieces with the deadly machete in the presence of the mothers and fathers themselves."

Senator John Sherman quoted at length from a Cuban book
describing ghastly atrocities committed by Weyler during the
earlier Ten Years' War (when Weyler was not even in Cuba)
and stating that the Spaniards had executed 43,500 Cubans
during that conflict.

Emotion, misinformation—those old ingredients of war—
were combined with a driving ambition (provoked by growth
and change) and capped with one of the most irresistible
forces of all: moral indignation! Could President McKinley
keep these powerful forces in check?

McKinley tried, but alas, he was, in truth, "weak, and a
bidder for the admiration of the crowd." Republican leaders,
correctly gauging the temper of a country stirred to frenzy
by a jingostic press, predicted political disaster unless the U.S.
intervened in Cuba. McKinley desperately wanted peace but,
like James Madison so long before him, could not withstand
the pressures for war.

Historians coldly analyzing the Spanish-American War from
the vantage point of years see it as the result of a shift in the
relative positions of two powers. The weaker one, Spain, could
not bear to face the painful truth and make realistic adjust-
ments. The Spaniards could have finessed the Americans by
instituting sweeping reforms in Cuba, thereby removing all
pretexts for going to war. But, like many nations, they strenu-
ously resisted all change.

Then, in the summer of 1897, the Spanish premier was
assassinated by an Italian anarchist, and more liberal forces
came into power. The new Spanish leadership began to in-
stitute all the necessary reforms, including Cuban self-government, but by then it was too late. The American people were
blinded with emotion.

In Cuba, these reforms provoked pro-Spanish riots, causing the American consul, Fitzhugh Lee, to fear for the safety of American citizens. Lee began issuing a stream of alarming cables, reporting rumors of "extensive and dangerous" anti-American conspiracies, and urging that "a strong naval force be concentrated off the Florida keys to move here at short notice."

Lee never specifically asked for the dispatch of warships to Cuba, and it was true that American citizens were in no real danger there. But the Administration was jittery and over-reacted. McKinley, concerned about being provocative, announced that since relations between Spain and the United States had improved, he would "resume the friendly naval visits at Cuban ports" which had been suspended at the outbreak of the revolution.

Accordingly, in January, 1898, the beautiful U.S.S. *Maine* steamed into Havana harbor, an act which one disgruntled American thought comparable to "waving a match in an oil well."

The *Maine* was cordially received by the local Spanish officials, and three peaceful weeks passed. Self-government was already operating in Cuba, and the sincerity and good intentions of the Spaniards appeared obvious.

Then suddenly, on the still tropical evening of February 15, 1898, the battleship *Maine* blew sky high at her mooring, in a gigantic explosion which shattered windows on shore, capsized small boats in the harbor and spewed out bodies and debris, "a perfect hail of flying iron."

The wreck burned furiously, emitting "a great column of fire" and touched off explosions of ammunition like rockets. It sank rapidly, its crew helplessly pinned in the twisted steel, screaming for help, a Catholic chaplain frantically telling them "to mention the name of Jesus, and again and again I repeated the absolution." Of 346 people on board, 266 perished.

Many of the survivors were in terrible condition. An American correspondent who reached a Havana hospital as the wounded were being brought in described a sailor "with his face blown away," a "lusty" marine crying, "For God's sake, let me die!" and a fireman who kept saying, "There is something in my eyes. . . . Wait and let me open them," when, in fact, his eyes were gone.

The American press could not be contained. "WAR! SURE!" screamed the New York *Journal*. "Maine Destroyed by Spanish."

McKinley did his best. He insisted that the explosion may have been an accident and appointed a court of inquiry to investigate. Everything depended on the court's findings. The members, all distinguished and conscientious, actually bent over backwards to find some indication of an internal explosion. They tirelessly sifted all the evidence they could gather from an examination of the wreck itself by divers and engineers, and from the testimony of survivors and eyewitnesses.

Meanwhile, events worked against the Spaniards. Senator Redfield Proctor of Vermont, a highly respected man, went to Cuba "skeptical" of the senational stories, and returned shaken, giving Congress a "dry, passionless, statistical recital" of Cuban suffering all the more effective for its lack of emotion. "Is is just as if Proctor had held up his right hand and sworn to it," observed one Congressman.

Senator Proctor described the *reconcentrados* as "torn from their homes, with foul earth, foul air, foul water and foul food or none; what wonder that one-half have died and that one-quarter of the living are so diseased that they can not be saved? . . . To me, the strongest appeal is not the barbarity practiced by Weyler nor the loss of the *Maine* . . . but the spectacle of a million and a half people, the entire native population of Cuba, struggling for freedom and deliverance from the worst misgovernment of which I have ever had knowledge."

All the more sensible people—those who had long doubted the irresponsible press and opposed war—now swung into line. "Senator Proctor's speech," commented the *Wall Street Journal* "converted a great many people in Wall Street, who have heretofore taken the ground that the United States had no business to interfere in a revolution on Spanish soil." And the American Banker, a firm opponent of war, could not understand, after reading Senator Proctor's report, "how anyone with a grain of human sympathy . . . can dispute the propriety of a policy of intervention, so only that this outraged people might be set free!"

When the naval court of inquiry finally released its findings, complete with technical details, Spain's fate was sealed. That august body had to conclude, after exhaustive investigation, that "the *Maine* was destroyed by the explosion of a submarine mine." (A second court of inquiry, held thirteen and a half years later when the ship was raised and re-examined, confirmed this finding.)

To the best of human knowledge, the *Maine* had been intentionally destroyed. But who had done it? Even today no one knows. Surely Spanish officials would never have sanctioned such a suicidal act. Acutely aware of their own weakness and the power of the United States, they were frantically trying to avoid a war. The only people who could have benefited were the insurgents themselves. But the American reaction was, "No matter who did it, if things are that bad in Cuba, then we should intervene."

Seldom have a people been so primed for war. It would have

taken a very strong President to buck them, and McKinley wasn't. He agonized and paced the floor, dispatching ultimatums to Madrid and praying for a miracle to deliver him from his predicament.

"Do you know what that white-livered cur up there has done?" raged Theodore Roosevelt, coming from the White House one evening. "He has prepared *two* messages, one for war and one for peace, and doesn't know which one to send in!" Clearly, in Roosevelt's own words, McKinley had "no more backbone than a chocolate éclair."

In Madrid, the American ambassador, Stewart Woodford, secured a complete capitulation to American demands: suspension of hostilities in Cuba, the revocation of reconcentration orders, a promise that Cuba's future would be left in the hands of its own autonomous government and an agreement to submit the *Maine* matter to arbitration. Ambassador Woodford thought that "this means peace, which the sober judgment of the people will approve long before next November, and which must be approved at the bar of final history."

If McKinley's prime goal had been the preservation of peace, these concessions would have been all he would have needed. But McKinley was chiefly concerned with quieting the public clamor, and nothing short of war could accomplish that.

Cabinet members found the President "nervous and terribly agitated," sleepless despite a resort to barbituates and no longer able to "think clearly." When talking to a friend, he "broke down and cried like a boy of thirteen." He finally gave up and turned the whole matter over to Congress. "But for the inflamed state of public opinion, and the fact that Congress could no longer be held in check," McKinley later admitted, "a peaceful solution might have been had."

The Speaker of the House, a firm opponent of war, put it

another way: "What's the use of being right when everyone else is wrong?" When urged by a state governor to somehow "dissuade" Congress, the Speaker (and he was known as "Czar" Reed) cried, "The Governor . . . might as well ask me to step out in the middle of a Kansas waste and dissuade a cyclone!"

"The scene upon the floor of the House resembled a political convention," an observer reported. "A half hundred of the Representatives gathered in the lobby in the rear of the hall and awoke the echoes with patriotic songs. 'The Battle Hymn of the Republic' was sung by General Henderson of Iowa, 'Dixie' and other songs were sung, led by some of the ex-Confederates, and then in tremendous volume the corridors rang with an improvisation: 'Hang General Weyler to a Sour Apple Tree as We Go Marching On!' "

Needless to say, the U.S. Congress declared war on Spain.

The country was thrilled. Democrats and Republicans, Northerners and Southerners, all joined hands in this noble crusade to free Cuba from the villainous Spaniards. So overcome was Congress with the magnanimity of the act that in the excitement it even passed a resolution (the Teller Amendment) disclaiming "any . . . intention to exercise sovereignty, jurisdiction, or control over said island [Cuba] except for the pacification thereof," and promising "when that is accomplished to leave the government and control of the island to its own people."

Spain was no match for the growing, pulsating United States. "We may and must expect a disaster," declared the commander of Spain's largest naval squadron as he resignedly went off to war. *"Pobre España!"*

In less than four months, the U.S. Navy destroyed the Spanish fleet, Atlantic and Pacific (with the loss of only seven American lives, one from heat stroke), and the U.S. Army, with only 365 battle deaths (but thousands more from disease), gained Cuba, Puerto Rico, Guam and Manila, crumbling the Spanish Empire.

"It has been a splendid little war," exulted John Hay, U.S. Ambassador to Great Britain, "begun with the highest motives, carried on with magnificent intelligence and spirit, favored by that fortune which loves the brave."

A "little war," to be sure, but one with profound consequences. Peace terms gave Cuba her independence, as promised, but transferred the islands of Guam, Puerto Rico and the Philippines to the United States. Overnight, America became a world power, owner of a colonial empire. Few Americans understood the tremendous changes they had wrought, or dreamed that they had inherited—along with their possessions —another war, longer and bloodier than the last, and hardly "splendid": the Philippine Insurrection.

VI

The Philippine Insurrection

The Philippine Insurrection was a direct legacy of the Spanish-American War. To understand how such a noble parent ("Free the Cubans!") could have sired such a wicked off-spring ("Conquer the Filipinos!"), one need only re-examine the strange mixture of altruism and national ambition which had fostered the Spanish-American War, and then add the desire for Chinese markets.

Competition for trade with China, a country of hundreds of millions of potential customers, was intense. England, Russia, France and Germany were actually carving that nation into exclusive spheres of influence and seizing its strategic ports.

With American trade so threatened, Commodore George Dewey's astonishing victory in Manila Bay at the beginning of the Spanish-American War seemed providential. Here, suddenly, was an Asiatic base for commercial operations in China!

"With the Philippines as a three-quarter way house, forming a superb training station," thought the New York *Commercial,* much of the rich Chinese trade "could come to this country."

"We are after markets," explained the *Forum,* "the greatest markets now existing in the world."

This powerful motive was strengthened by simple national pride. Many Americans found it thrilling to own property. "Our war in aid of Cuba has assumed undreamed of dimensions," observed the pleased Philadelphia *Record.* "Willy nilly we have entered upon our career as a world power."

And if having a colonial empire was difficult to reconcile with basic American principles, it could always be excused as a "missionary "enterprise. Americans, with their special genius for government, had a *duty,* they decided, to carry "political civilization" into "those parts of the world inhabited by unpolitical and barbaric races." It was their "white man's burden."

Not all Americans agreed, for the country's anticolonial tradition was strong. Republicans tended to support an expansionist policy ("manifest destiny in its broadest sense"), but many Democrats thought it ironic that America had gone to war to destroy a colonial power only to become one herself.

President McKinley, albeit a Republican, shared these misgivings. He deplored "territorial aggression."

"The truth is I didn't want the Philippines, and when they came to us, as a gift from the gods, I did not know what to do with them," he later confessed. "I walked the floor of the White House night after night . . . and I am not ashamed to tell you, gentlemen, that I went down on my knees and prayed Almighty God for light and guidance more than one night. And one night it came to me this way: (1) that we could not give them back to Spain—that would be cowardly and dishonorable; (2) that we could not turn them over to France or Germany, our commercial rivals in the Orient—that would be bad business and discreditable; (3) that we could not leave them to themselves—they are unfit for self-government . . . ; and (4) that there was nothing left for us to do but to take them all, and to educate the Filipinos and uplift and civilize and Christianize them, and by God's grace to do the best we could by them . . . And then I went to bed . . . and slept soundly, and the next morning I sent for . . . our map maker and told him to put the Philippines on the map of the United States . . . and there they are, and there they will stay while I am president!"

Unfortunately, all of President McKinley's assumptions were erroneous. First, Americans did not even possess the islands. They had destroyed some antiquated Spanish vessels in Manila Bay and then, with the aid of thousands of Filipino soldiers, had captured *from the Spanish* the inner city of old Manila—a far cry from acquiring *from the Filipinos* the whole archipelago, land comprising more square miles than all of New England and New York combined. Nor could the islands be "given" back to Spain. America did not have them to give, and Spain probably did not have the power to reconquer them.

McKinley's assumption that the Filipinos were in need of "Christianizing" was patently absurd. Almost all of the Filipino people were Christians and had been for over 300 years. (The Moros were an obvious exception, but they would give American missionaries as much trouble as they gave the Spanish.)

The President's statement that the Filipinos, whom he had never met, were "unfit for self-government" was equally ignorant. Like most provincial Americans, McKinley just naturally assumed that any natives that unknown and that far away were, of course, uncivilized. Reports to the contrary failed to penetrate. "We have . . . underrated the natives," one American general tried to tell the War Department. "They are not ignorant savage tribes, but have a civilization of their own." Even Commodore Dewey believed that the Filipinos were "superior in intelligence and more capable of self-government than the natives of Cuba, and I am familiar with both races." Carl Schurz, a noted politician, conceded that a Filipino government might be "far from perfect," but tried to point out that "the conduct of no people is perfect. . . . We, too, have had our civil war which cost hundreds and thousands of lives and devastated one-half of our land; and now we have in horrible abundance the killings by lynch law. . . . They may have troubles with their wild tribes. So had we, and we treated our wild tribes in a manner not to be proud of. They may have corruption and rapacity in their government, but . . . not much less virtuous than that of Chicago."

But none are so blind as those who will not see. The idea that the Filipinos were "unfit for self-government" took deep root in the American mind. Nourished by constant repetition in the press, it became dogma, parroted by everyone.

Few Americans knew that the Filipino people had risen against their Spanish oppressors in 1896. The Spaniards, realizing that hostilities might continue for years, had signed a pact, promising amnesty to all Filipinos who laid down their arms, agreeing to pay an indemnity of $850,000 and permitting the rebel leader, handsome young Emilio Aguinaldo, safe exile in Hong Kong. There was also an understanding that some badly needed reforms would be instituted.

The reforms never came, many ex-insurgents were arrested

and only a small portion of the indemnity was paid. Consequently, violence continued to flare throughout the islands.

"Conditions here and in Cuba are practically alike," the U.S. Consul in Manila had reported two months before the Spanish-American War began. "War exists; and battles are of almost daily occurrence. Prisoners are brought here and shot without trial, and Manila is under martial law. . . . Insurgents are being armed and drilled, are rapidly increasing in number and efficiency, and all agree that a general uprising will come."

Emilio Aguinaldo was planning to return from Hong Kong to lead the rebellion. While he was making preparations, he and his aides became increasingly aware of the presence in that British port of the American Asiatic Squadron. News of the sinking of the *Maine,* with all its implications, greatly excited these Filipinos, giving them their first realistic hope of success. In informal talks with American naval officers, they received the impression that if America fought with Spain, the Philippines would be given their independence. "The United States, my general, is a great and rich nation, and neither needs nor desires colonies," the commander of the U.S.S. *Petrel* supposedly told Aguinaldo.

Once the Spanish-American War began, the American consuls, both in Hong Kong and in Singapore, where Aguinaldo spent some time, urged Aguinaldo to return to the Phillipines to lead his people in insurrection.

"What can we expect to gain from helping America?" the wary rebel leader asked.

"Independence," replied one consul, and apparently he was sincere. He told Aguinaldo about the Teller Amendment, in which Congress had disclaimed any desire to possess Cuba. "As in Cuba, so in the Philippines. Even more so, if possible;

Cuba is at our door while the Philippines are 10,000 miles away!"

The possibilities were too enormous to be disregarded. Pinning his hopes on the Teller Amendment, Aguinaldo issued a dramatic proclamation to his people:

"Compatriots! Divine Province is about to place independence within our reach. Americans, not from mercenary motives, but for the sake of humanity and the lamentations of so many persecuted people, have considered it opportune to extend their protecting mantle to our beloved country. . . . The Americans will attack by sea. . . . We insurgents must attack by land. . . . Where you see the American flag flying, assemble in numbers; they are our redeemers!"

After Dewey's fantastic victory in Manila Bay, the U.S.S. *McCulloch* returned to Hong Kong to get Aguinaldo. News of Aguinaldo's return spread through the islands. He "could have had any number of men," according to Dewey, "it was just a question of arming them." Indeed, Aguinaldo could have had the "whole population."

Dewey helped supply arms, and then told Aguinaldo, "Well, now, . . . go ashore there and start your army." With only 1,743 men, Dewey could no more than blockade the bay. While awaiting the arrival of American land forces from San Francisco, he (in his own words) made "use of him [Aguinaldo] and the natives to assist me in the operations against the Spaniards."

The Filipinos defeated the Spaniards in one engagement after another, capturing province after province, until they controlled the entire major island of Luzon with the exception of Manila. They then advanced relentlessly toward that capital, seizing one suburb after another and forcing thousands of

Spanish troops to fall back behind the ancient walls. By the end of June, 1898, the Filipinos had built fourteen miles of trenches around Manila's Walled City and captured its pumping plant, severing the water supply.

In the meantime, they drew up and proclaimed to all the world a dramatic Declaration of Independence—an event celebrated with wild rejoicing throughout the islands. The new flag was unfurled, the new national anthem played and the republic launched under the first democratic constitution ever known in Asia.

But there were clouds in the infant nation's sky. The arrival of American expeditionary forces—11,000 by the end of July— was extremely disquieting. Since Aguinaldo thought that his men could have easily captured Manila with the aid of Dewey's naval guns, he could not understand "whom the Americans expected to fight."

"Does the United States intend to hold the Philippines as dependencies?" he bluntly asked General Thomas Anderson.

Startled, Anderson replied, "I cannot answer that, but in 122 years we have established no colonies. . . . I leave you to draw your own inferences."

"Situation difficult," General Wesley Merritt warned the War Department. "Insurgents have announced independent government; some are unfriendly." The Americans might need more troops to "hold insurgents while we fight Spaniards."

This first hint of trouble with the Filipinos was duly reported in the American press. "INSURGENTS NOT OUR ALLIES," proclaimed *The New York Times*. "Aguinaldo, the Rebel Leader of the Philippines, Has Grown Arrogant, and Is a Hindrance."

The Spaniards, hopelessly besieged in Manila, sought to

make the best of a dreadful situation by negotiating with the Americans. Their prime concern was to escape the wrath of the native army. If the Americans would keep out the Filipinos (*"los diablos negros"*), the Spaniards would surrender the city—after a token "battle" to preserve the honor of Spain.

Dewey accordingly ordered the Filipinos not to advance, under pain of being shelled by the U.S.S. *Petrel*. "Do not let your troops enter Manila without the permission of the American commander," General Anderson wired Aguinaldo. "On this side of the Pasig River you will be under our fire."

A sham battle was staged, Manila duly fell and American forces marched in. The Filipinos, denied entry to their capital city, were almost wild with outrage and fury.

From that moment on, relations between the Americans and Filipinos degenerated into war. The Filipino troops refused to withdraw from the environs of Manila. They kept the Americans hemmed in, surrounded. Incidents mounted. Under such circumstances, war was inevitable—unless the Americans were willing to recognize the independence of the Filipino people.

Here history provides a classic example of the role ignorance plays in bringing on a conflict. If Americans had had any knowledge of the actual situation in the Philippines, they would have known that they could not possibly possess those islands without brutally conquering the people.

The consuming desire for a foothold in Asia was obscuring all reality. "We hold the other side of the Pacific," Senator Henry Cabot Lodge excitedly wrote a friend, "and the value to this country is almost beyond recognition." No matter what, "we must not let the Islands go. . . . They must be ours under the treaty of peace."

"Fact-finding" commissions dispatched to the Philippines interviewed the wrong people—primarily wealthy Spaniards in Manila—and found only what they wanted to find. Warnings that American rule would mean war with the insurgents were totally disregarded. American high officials had acquired the fantastic notion that the insurgents represented only 0.5 per cent of the Philippine population, and they clung to this fairy tale despite continuing and overwhelming evidence to the contrary. McKinley always believed that American rule was desired by "the great masses of the Filipino people"—despite reports from Americans who had actually traveled through the provinces that "on one point they [the people] seem united, viz., that whatever our government may have done for them, it had not gained the right to annex them."

(When the Philippine Insurrection was in full swing and it was obvious that the entire native population was in arms—"There are no *amigos*," American soldiers quickly learned—that America could not conquer without burning all villages, occupying *every* town and reconcentrating the people, Weyler style, into those garrisoned units and that these conditions existed on all the islands, McKinley actually told the American people that there was no "Philippine nation" but rather "more than sixty tribes . . . all but one ready to accept American sovereignty.")

Against such ignorance, the Filipinos were powerless. Aguinaldo sent his representative, Don Felipe Agoncillo, to Washington to speak directly with President McKinley. McKinley listened politely to the Filipino, but refused his request to be represented at the Paris peace talks, where the fate of the Philippines would be decided.

Nevertheless, Agoncillo went to Paris, where he found all doors closed to him. When the peace treaty was finally completed on December 10, 1898, and the Philippine Islands duly transferred to the United States, a heartbroken Agoncillo could do no more than officially protest, declaring the treaty "not binding" upon his government, since "the commission did not hear the Filipino people."

Agoncillo then returned to Washington, where he tried to alert the Secretary of State to the extremely explosive situation in the Philippines. But the State Department was blind to any impending trouble. The Américan Philippine commander, General Ewell Otis, who busied himself with unnecessary paper work in his office in Manila and seldom saw beyond his own walls, was cheerfully reporting that all was well. The State Department refused to even answer Agoncillo's messages, much less see him.

But war was coming, and those on the scene knew it. Two large armies—American and Filipino—faced each other in constant abrasion from the capture of Manila on August 13, 1898, until the outbreak of hostilities on February 4, 1899. During those six months, tension mounted until it became almost unbearable.

Taunts and obscenities were exchanged across the lines, the dividing neutral zone was repeatedly violated, Filipinos were contemptuously shot and Americans were kidnaped and sometimes knifed.

Hostilities began one dark moonless night after two American soldiers—part of a unit that had been foolishly advanced into insurgent territory—shot and killed three Filipinos who appeared to be penetrating their lines. Nerves by that time were so taut that the slightest provocation brought instant overreaction. The Americans heard a whistle, answered by another, and saw a flashing red light. "Line up, fellows," they cried, "The niggers are in here all through these yards." Firing broke out and spread along a ten-mile front. A full-scale battle was soon in progress.

War was never declared. Americans just suddenly found themselves, to their dismay, in a conflict thousands of miles from their shores—a ghastly, brutal affair that consumed far more dollars and lives than the Spanish-American War.

One and all were appalled. "Destiny," observed William Jennings Bryan, "is not as manifest as it was a few weeks ago."

The fighting promised to be endless, with military commanders continually insisting that the next campaign would be the last. While it was true that the Filipinos, armed with ancient weapons and always lacking ammunition, were no match for the Americans, with their navy, their deadly Hotchkiss and Gatling machine guns, telescopic sights and heavy artillery, their effort was total ("Everyone was against us," an American general later grumbled), and their resistance inspired. Defeated on the battlefield, they turned to guerrilla warfare. Their subjugation became a mammoth project, requiring more than four times the number of troops that had fought in Cuba during the Spanish-American War. Although every island was systematically crisscrossed, four hundred garrisons established and all civilians rounded up into concentration areas (where they died from disease and starvation), violence still persisted. What was crushed in one spot popped up in another.

Both sides committed unspeakable atrocities. American prisoners were tortured, mutilated and buried alive. "Last night one of our boys was found shot and his stomach cut open," wrote a private. "Immediately orders were received . . .

to burn the town and kill every native in sight; which was done."

Americans wantonly destroyed property, looted churches, tortured prisoners with the terrible "water cure" and killed countless women and children. Some men were shocked enough to bring formal charges against their own officers ("that he did maliciously, wilfully, and without just cause, shoot and kill an unarmed prisoner of war on his knees before him, begging for life . . ."), but the army repeatedly decided that "public policy" required that "no further action be taken." Two officers were finally court-martialed—one was a general who had ordered the island of Samar turned into a "howling wilderness," with the slaughter of "all persons over the age of ten" in retaliation for a hideous massacre of American soldiers. "I want no prisoners. . . . The more you kill and burn, the better it will please me."

When civilian deaths topped 200,000, Americans had come full circle—having gone to war against Spain in 1898 to stop just such barbarities. "The good Lord in Heaven only knows the number of Filipinos that were put under ground," a Congressman ruefully mused after a visit to Manila. "Our soldiers took no prisoners, they kept no records; they simply swept the country, and wherever and whenever they could get hold of a Filipino they killed him." Filipino casualties were higher than they would be against the Japanese in World War II.

Strict censorship deterred correspondents from reporting these appalling facts. "Of course we all know that we are in a terrible mess out here," a staff aide confided, "but we don't want the folks to get excited about it. If you fellows will only keep quiet now we will pull through in time."

A complete muzzling was impossible, however, and shocking

stories finally drifted back to the states. Many Americans were horrified. Opposition to the war skyrocketed, with sentiment polarizing along the political lines. Republicans, while distressed, generally maintained that "the flag cannot be lowered," American prestige was at stake and rebellion could not be tolerated (the British view in 1775). "The first blow was struck by the inhabitants," McKinley kept saying. He was still baffled that the Filipinos were so ungratefully "shooting down their rescuers." But the horrified Democrats insisted that, no matter what, this war "against liberty" was unjust and should cease.

After three years Filipino resistance finally received a mortal blow with the capture of Aguinaldo (an exploit that involved the use of torture to learn his whereabouts and trickery to infiltrate his stronghold). Fighting still persisted, and remote American garrisons were massacred as late as 1916, but the rebellion was, for all purposes, crushed. The proud Philippine Republic was ground into dust, its Declaration of Independence and Constitution (patterned after the American models) consigned to history.

This sorry venture into imperialism sickened the American people. To ease their guilt, they made the Philippines their special missionary project. They poured dollars into the islands—building roads, bridges, schools and hospitals. Doctors, nurses, school teachers and engineers offered their services. Dread diseases were brought under control. The standard of living soared. A Filipino legislature was inaugurated, and the first steps taken toward eventual self-government.

The United States conducted the most benevolent colonial government in history. When it finally granted the Philippine

Islands complete independence in 1946, it was the world's first colonial power to voluntarily take such action.

Nevertheless, the subjugation of those people was a dreadful wrong and the war a terrible mistake.

"If only Dewey had sailed away after he smashed the Spanish fleet," President McKinley finally decided, "What a lot of trouble he would have saved us." If only President McKinley had been properly informed, what a grisly war he might have averted.

VII

World War I

In the summer of 1914, the entire continent of Europe burst into war. The world had never seen anything like it. The assassination of Archduke Francis Ferdinand, the heir to the Austrian throne, while on a visit to Serbia, triggered a complete collapse of European civilization. Every major power simultaneously combusted.

Americans, ignorant of the forces which for two generations had been building toward that titanic eruption, thought that it had come "as lightning out of a clear sky." The more knowledgeable were aware of the national ambitions and rampaging hatreds and fears that had split the continent into two camps, so tense and overarmed that any incident could ignite a war.

Thus Austria sought to punish Serbia for the assassination; Russia defended the little country; Germany backed Austria, declaring war on Russia and on France (France being tied by treaty to Russia), and then invaded Belgium to get at France, bringing England, which had solemnly guaranteed Belgium's neutrality, into the war. With a few weeks the Ottoman Empire joined Germany and Austria-Hungary, and a great conflagration was raging.

The brilliant, scholarly American President, Woodrow Wilson, saw it as a "natural raking out of the pent-up jealousies and rivalries of the complicated politics of Europe." It was "a war with which we have nothing to do, whose causes cannot touch us." He proclaimed American neutrality, asking his people to be "impartial in thought as well as in action."

Americans could be impartial "in action," but they could not control their thoughts. From almost the very beginning, they sympathized with the Allied powers, most particularly Britain and France. (Among the exceptions were numerous German-Americans, whose emotional ties to their fatherland were strong, and many Irish, who were intensely anti-British.)

Austria's harsh ultimatum to little Serbia struck most Americans as bullying and provocative. Germany's hasty declarations of war made her appear the aggressor, while her invasion of Belgium was shocking in the extreme—a bold violation of sacred European treaties guaranteeing Belgium's neutrality in perpetuity. The ruthless conquest of that small and helpless nation was bad enough, but Germany's curt dismissal of her treaty as "just a scrap of paper" suggested a return to barbarism which was especially repugnant in those idealistic times, when people strove to be "gentlemen" and a man's word was always golden. The fact that Belgium chose to fight a hopeless battle against her invaders aroused the admiration of almost every American, while the multitudinous stories of German atrocities in Belgium—the deliberate destruction of towns and cathedrals, the deportation of men for slave labor, the shooting of priests and civilian hostages—affronted the moral sense of the nation. (Even the German chief of staff had to admit that "our advance in Belgium is certainly brutal.") The German Ambassador to the United States reported after the war: "The Belgium question was the one which interested Americans the most, and which was most effective in working up American public opinion against us."

Stripped to its nub, the European war was a power struggle. England had reigned supreme for a hundred years, since the fall of Napoleon. Her great navy controlled the seas; her influence disciplined the world. The rise of Germany in the mid-1800s under Prussian militarists was a direct challenge—one that intensified as German strength and ambitions grew. A German triumph over France in 1870, the growth of a great German navy, an expanding German colonial empire, greater German commercial competition—these developments were disquieting, to say the least, and not just to France and Great Britain. Americans, in an enlarged world community, identified with the British as kinsmen, sharing the same language and ideals. Their interests were closely intertwined. Americans felt safe as long as the British controlled the Atlantic. Any threat to British naval supremacy, and especially from a power as aggressive and militaristic as Germany, was bound to make Americans uneasy. As the war progressed, with the Germans appearing increasingly barbarous, most Americans became convinced that a German victory would be disastrous. As Rudyard Kipling so movingly put it, "What stands if Freedom fall? Who dies if England live?"

The last thing Americans wanted, however, was to become

involved. The war was a horror—the greatest bloodbath the world had ever known, with new and terrible weapons inflicting death, torture, invalidism and destruction on a scale never before envisioned. "The ferocity of it . . . passes anything felt by any men in modern times," the U.S. Ambassador to England wrote President Wilson. "All preceding mere 'wars' are not in the same class of events."

Half a million men were killed during the siege of Verdun ("What scenes of horror and carnage! . . . Hell cannot be so terrible!"), over a million (twice the death toll of the entire American Civil War) in five months of futile attacks and counterattacks along the river Somme. "This isn't war!" gasped a horrified British minister, veteran of many older, bloody battles.

Americans were aghast at the thought of sending their youths into such slaughter. *"I didn't raise my boy to be a soldier,"* proclaimed a tin-pan alley song, especially popular among American women,

> *I brought him up to be my pride and joy!*
> *Who dares to place a musket on his shoulder*
> *To shoot some other mother's darling boy?*

Theoretically, Americans should have been able to stay out of a power struggle three thousand miles from their shores, but they encountered the same problem as in 1812: how to trade with a world at war. America was a major producing nation; foreign commerce was essential to her life processes.

Great Britain's superior fleet swept German ships from the seas and instituted a tight blockade, preventing the United States from trading with Britain's enemies. It was 1812 all over again, complete with irritating Orders-in-Council, but this time the British were duly respectful; they did not seize ships without compensation or impress sailors. Besides, the Americans suffered no hardship, for increased British and French buying more than compensated for the loss of the central European market. In two years, U.S. wheat exports skyrocketed from $89 million to $333 million, U.S. munitions sales soared beyond a staggering $1½ billion. The profits of Bethlehem Steel almost tripled in one year; meat-packing profits doubled; one small firm's production rose 1,605 per cent. The American people were enjoying an unprecedented, galloping prosperity as the Allies became more and more dependent on their products. The United States was soon the Allies' breadbasket and arsenal—indeed, the Allies' only hope of defeating powerful Germany.

Germany naturally resented this one-sided American aid. She attacked it with the most effective weapon at her disposal, the new and terrible submarine.

Submarine warfare, by its very nature, meant sneak attacks, "without it always being possible to warn the crews and passengers" (official German notice). This fact is clearly understood in today's more callous world, but in 1915 it violated accepted traditions of civilized naval warfare, and people were outraged.

President Wilson understood that "the conditions of war had radically changed," but insisted that "the rules had not." He warned Germany that if her U-boats destroyed American ships *or* American lives, the United States would hold her to "a strict accountability." Considerable discussion ensued in Washington as to whether Americans should be forbidden to travel on belligerent ships in order to avoid incidents. Wilson vigorously opposed such a restriction. "I cannot consent to any abridgement of the right of American citizens in any respect," he insisted. His reasoning seemed sound: "Once accept a single abatement of right, and many other humiliations would certainly follow." But compared with the extremes resorted to by the United States to stay out of World War II, Wilson's stand appears almost provocative. It placed his country in the position of having to fight to defend its neutral rights—a contradiction, if ever there was one.

It was only a matter of time before Americans traveling on foreign ships would be killed. Late in March, 1915, a German U-boat sank the British liner *Falaba* in the Irish Sea. One hundred and four people were lost, including an American.

Several weeks later the great British four-stack luxury liner *Lusitania*, which had sailed from New York, was torpedoed without warning off the Irish coast. This pride of the Cunard line sank in an incredible eighteen minutes. Of the almost 2,000 passengers aboard, only 764 were saved. The dead included 128 Americans, many of them women and children. (One photograph, circulated in the newspapers, depicted a dead woman clutching an infant corpse in each arm.) This tragedy "literally overwhelmed America," Secretary of War Newton Baker wrote later, "and public opinion never recovered from it." The torpedoing of a huge unarmed *passenger* vessel, with the consequent loss of almost 1,200 noncombatants, seemed like deliberate, wholesale murder. The fact that the *Lusitania* was carrying 4,200 cases of small arms made no difference; the widespread impression of German barbarism was confirmed. Americans were now certain that that "nation of the black hand and bloody heart" was a threat to civilization itself. A German victory in Europe would mean "the overthrow of democracy in the world . . . [and] the turning back of the hands of human progress two centuries."

As the sinking of passenger ships continued, with the loss of American lives, President Wilson rode the tide of his countrymen's anger, staunchly refusing to be pressured by a vocal minority clamoring for war. (Ex-President Theodore Roosevelt attributed 'the murder of the thousand men, women and children on the Lusitania . . . solely [to] Wilson's abject cowardice and weakness" and deplored the fact that Wilson would not go to war unless "kicked into it." And on second thought, perhaps not even then: "If anyone kicks him he brushes his clothes and utters some lofty sentence.")

Actually, the *Lusitania*'s sinking hung on Wilson "like a terrible nightmare," causing him "many sleepless hours," but he steeled himself against an emotional reaction. He went into seclusion, realizing that he would "see red in everything" and "probably not be just to anyone" if he let his mind dwell on "the tragic details in the newspapers." After several days he emerged to announce, undoubtedly to snorts from Roosevelt, that "peace is a healing and elevating influence . . . and strife is not. There is such a thing as a man being too proud to fight. There is such a thing as a nation being so right that it does not need to convince others by force that it is right."

Wilson's distaste for war, however, did not stop him from dealing firmly with Germany. He was a man of steel, especially when it came to principles. To Wilson, the attacks on unarmed passenger ships were flagrant violations of international law, "utterly incompatible with the principles of humanity." He saw the submarine as an atrocious instrument, "which it is impossible to employ . . . in accordance with any rules that the world is likely to be willing to accept." In April, 1916, he informed the German Government that unless it "immediately" declared and effected "an abandonment of its present methods of submarine warfare against passenger and freight-carrying vessels," the United States would "have no choice but to sever diplomatic relations."

The German Government, alarmed by the hornet's nest it had aroused in the United States, acquiesced—a tremendous diplomatic victory for President Wilson. It accepted liability in the death of neutrals from U-boat attacks and promised henceforth to confine its activities "to the fighting forces of the belligerents," while assuring that merchant vessels "shall not be sunk without warning and without saving human lives. . . ."

The United States breathed a sigh of relief. German-American relations improved perceptibly.

But not for long. The Germans now attempted to destroy the Allies' munitions sources by another means: sabotage.

Early in the morning of July 30, 1916, a tremendous explosion rocked New York harbor, shaking bridges over the East River, shattering windows as far north as 42nd Street, and raining shrapnel upon lower Manhattan. The tremor was felt as far away as Baltimore. Black Tom Island, a major shipping station for munitions to Europe, had blown up. Damage was set at $22 million.

The Black Tom explosion was only the first of many attributed to the Germans. Time bombs were planted on ships about to sail for Allied ports. Strikes were fomented among longshoremen and munitions workers. The Canadian Car and Foundry plant at Kingland, New Jersey, was destroyed. The Congress Street docks in Brooklyn were set on fire, with the loss of twelve vessels and their adjoining piers.

Irrefutable evidence of German sabotage began to unfold everywhere. U.S. secret agents learned, through captured documents, that before the end of 1915, Germany had spent $27 million on propaganda and espionage in the United States.

In fairness to Germany, it should be said that she was desperate. President Wilson had all but neutralized the one weapon—the U-boat—that had given her any real hope of victory. The Germans were understandably angry over America's "favoritism" in forcing Germany to adhere to principles of international law while accepting Britain's clearly illegal and inhuman "starvation" blockade.

It was true that President Wilson's sympathies were with the British, but he nevertheless strove to remain impartial "against heavy difficulties" (his own words). He vigorously protested Britain's arbitrary blockade; indeed, his indignant notes were reminiscent of James Madison's in the five years before the War of 1812.

"We must . . . put a curb on our sentiments," he insisted. His own self-enforced objectivity was seen in his continual attempts to negotiate an end to the war—attempts which were, according to the German Ambassador in Washington, "unwaveringly adhered to until the rupture."

When the conflict first began, Wilson offered his services as mediator, but as his close aide, Colonel Edward House, discovered when he sounded out the belligerent nations, "Everyone wants peace, but nobody is willing to concede enough to get it." Wilson kept trying. On his third attempt, late in 1916, he announced himself as "the friend of all nations engaged in the present struggle" and asked the governments to state their war aims—"the precise objects which would . . . satisfy them and their people that the war had been fought out." But the Allies were furious that Wilson would morally equate them with their enemies. France announced her goals as "victory"; Britain's terms included "complete restitution" and "full reparation"; and Germany's territorial demands were so extreme that the German chancellor did not even dare state them.

Early in 1917, Wilson tried to force the issue by stating the sort of settlement which *he* thought the belligerents should be seeking. In a magnificent speech before the U.S. Senate, he depicted a great new world, embracing principles of self-government, arms control and freedom of the seas, policed by "the organized major force of mankind." He urged the termination of the war by compromise—a "peace without victory," without humiliation, a negotiated peace between equals. "A victor's terms imposed upon the vanquished," he warned prophetically, "would leave a sting, a resentment, a bitter memory, upon which terms of peace would rest, not permanently, but only as upon quicksand."

But the nations of Europe had suffered too much to settle for anything short of victory. The British prime minister informed Wilson that "the people of this country do not believe that peace can be durable unless it is based on the success of the Allies." The war would have to be fought almost to the bitter end.

The climax was nearing. The great powers were exhausted, bled white, searching for any way to end the deadlock before they themselves expired. Desperate to break the blockade which was starving their people, German leaders decided to resume unrestricted submarine warfare.

It was a terrible gamble. It would almost certainly bring America into the war. But the Germans hoped, by ruthlessly sinking *every* vessel approaching Great Britain, to have that nation "gasping in the reeds like a fish" before America could get her forces into the arena. Besides, German leaders (then and, incredibly, again in 1941) grossly underestimated America's military potential. "The assistance which will result from the entrance of the United States into the war," they thought, "will amount to nothing."

And so began the sinking of American ships which finally forced Woodrow Wilson's hand.

When the Germans announced, On January 31, 1917, that they would henceforth sink on sight ships of *any* nation found within a broad area designated as a "war zone," the President was appalled. His dilemma was absolute. Theoretically he could avoid war by keeping American vessels off the seas, but in practice such action was unthinkable. Jefferson's disastrous Embargo in 1808, when the country was infinitely smaller, had clearly dramatized the dangers of restricting American trade. In 1917, with the economy enormously expanded and industry operating in highest gear, such a move would have brought economic disaster. And there was an even more powerful factor: Great Britain and France had to have American products to live, and Americans desperately did not want those two great democracies to die. The salvation of Britain and France, they thought, was essential to America's own safety. Thus they had a vital interest in the outcome of the war—a tricky position for any neutral nation to be in.

On February 3, 1917, President Wilson reluctantly broke diplomatic relations with Germany. "There was nothing else for the United States to do," sighed the German Ambassador as he was handed his passport.

Two months of tense "watchful waiting" followed, with Wilson hoping against hope that the Germans did not intend "to do in fact what they have warned us they feel at liberty to do." Wilson insisted that it would be "a crime" to go to war if it was humanly possible to avoid it. "I am doing everything that I honorably can to keep the country out of war," he wrote.

Then came three dramatic events which pushed America over the brink:

The first was the discovery of a shocking communication from the German foreign minister, Arthur Zimmerman, to the Mexican Government which was intercepted and decoded by the British and obligingly relayed to the United States: "WE INTEND TO BEGIN UNRESTRICTED SUBMARINE WARFARE. . . . WE SHALL ENDEAVOR IN SPITE OF THIS TO KEEP THE UNITED STATES NEUTRAL. IN THE EVENT OF THIS NOT SUCCEEDING, WE MAKE MEXICO A PROPOSAL OF ALLIANCE ON THE FOLLOWING BASIS: MAKE WAR TOGETHER, MAKE PEACE TOGETHER, GENEROUS FINANCIAL SUPPORT, AND AN UNDERSTANDING ON OUR PART THAT MEXICO IS TO RECONQUER THE LOST TERRITORY IN TEXAS, NEW MEXICO AND ARIZONA. . . ." The Mexican Government was further urged to "invite Japan" to defect from the Allies and join this alliance.

The impact of this "Zimmerman Note" on President Wilson, and on American public opinion, can hardly be exaggerated, suggesting as it did the stirring up of "enemies against us at our very doors," the loss of precious land and war on America's own soil. This "Prussian Invasion Plot" united the people from coast to coast, bringing visions of "hordes of Mexicans under German officers, sweeping into Texas, New Mexico and Arizona." The Cleveland *Plain Dealer* saw "neither virtue nor dignity" in remaining neutral any longer. "The issue shifts," declared the Omaha *World Herald,* "from Germany against Great Britain to Germany against the United States." Wrote Roosevelt, "If Wilson does not go to war now, I shall skin him alive."

The second dramatic event was a revolution in Russia. Russia, a great ally of Britain and France, had been in the war from the beginnng, but Americans had never been able to identify with that autocratic power. They had had little interest in the fighting on the eastern front, bloody and protracted though it was. When the astounding news came in March that the Czar had abdicated and a coaliton government had been established in Petrograd, the entire complexion of the war cleared. Now the conflict could be viewed distinctly as a struggle between democracy and tyranny. The "wonderful and heartening" (Wilson's words) overthrow of the Czar had removed the only taint from the Allied cause, converting Russia into "a fit partner for a League of Honor."

Finally, the sinking of Amercan ships, one after another, left little choice but to go to war. As in 1812, the position of a large neutral in a torn world was untenable. "There is no question about going to war," declared ex-President Roosevelt. "Germany is already at war with us." On March 12, the unarmed American ship *Algonquin* went down in British waters. On March 18, the *City of Memphis,* the *Illinois* and the *Vigilancia* were all torpedoed without warning and with heavy loss of life, followed by the American freighter *Aztec.*

Meanwhile, reports were arriving that the Allies' situation was desperate; in France, soldiers were deserting by the thousands; only direct American intervention could save the day.

Public sentiment was now completely aroused, but Wilson

was no McKinley. "I want to be right whether it is popular or not," he insisted.

He stayed up the entire night of April 1-2, unburdening himself to Frank Cobb, editor of the New York *World*. "Once lead this people into war," he groaned, "and they'll forget there ever was such a thing as tolerance. To fight, you must be brutal and ruthless." They talked until dawn. "If there is any alternative," Wilson kept saying, "for God's sake, let's take it."

There seemed to be none—not unless the United States was willing to share the world, and the seas, with a triumphant, dangerously aggressive Germany.

At eight o'clock in the evening of April 2, 1917, a grave and haggard Woodrow Wilson, his hands shaking as he turned the pages of his speech, asked Congress for a declaration of war. "Neutrality is no longer feasible or desirable when the peace of the world is involved and the freedom of its peoples," he declared, explaining that "the menace to that peace and freedom lies in the existence of autocratic governments, backed by organized force which is controlled wholly by their will, not by the will of their people."

Proudly he stated, "We have no selfish ends to serve. We desire no conquest, no dominion. We seek no indemnities for ourselves, no material compensation for the sacrifices we shall freely make." It all boiled down to one thing: "The world must be made safe for democracy."

The President recognized that "it is a fearful thing to lead this great and peaceful people into war, into the most terrible and disastrous of all wars, civilization itself seeming to be in the balance." "But," he added, "the right is more precious than peace. . . . The day has come when America is privileged to spend her blood and her might for the principles that gave her birth and happiness and the peace which she has treasured. Got helping her, she can do no other."

He received a standing ovation.

"My message today was a message of death to our young men," he commented sadly to his secretary. "How strange that they should applaud."

Having led his people into "the most terrible and disastrous of all wars," Woodrow Wilson felt compelled to elevate the venture. Under his inspired leadership, it became a great crusade for freedom, the likes of which the world had never seen.

Americans sincerely believed that this war was different from all others, that it was a war which would end all wars and make the world safe for democracy. "I never saw such innocence as I saw in their eyes those first months after America entered the war," declared a former British prime minister. Here was the climax to America's historic mission.

Americans gave it everything. It was the first total effort since the Civil War, conscripting all men of military age. Civilians enthusiastically pitched in, buying liberty bonds, cultivating home gardens, enduring heatless, wheatless, meatless and lightless days. Women became war workers, farmers, trolley conductors and cab drivers in order to release men for military service. The country was engulfed in a wave of emotional patriotism, sustained by speeches, parades and songs.

"Tell your Americans to come quickly," the French premier urged a newspaperman. "A terrible blow is imminent." The Allies' position was desperate. Italy, fighting on their side, collapsed in October after an Austro-German breakthrough at Caporetto; its army was in full retreat. Russian forces had already disintegrated—a result of the March revolution. Then, in November, the Bolsheviks, led by Nikolai Lenin, seized control of the government and began separate peace negotiations with Germany, thus releasing one million seasoned German troops for the western front.

The United States stepped up its training, and by April, 1918, American soldiers were finally pouring into Europe in huge numbers. The total reached an astounding two million. This new and seemingly endless supply of fresh, cheerful, well-equipped men was a lifesaving shot in the arm to the exhausted Allies. It tipped the scales for victory.

Another great American contribution was the idealistic leadership of Woodrow Wilson. Wilson's eloquent words were continual shafts of light in the darkness, giving meaning to a terrible war. They lifted disheartened souls everywhere, offering the first real hope for a better world.

In January, 1918, Wilson had enunciated his famous Fourteen Points as a basis for settling the war. This document, later supplemented, included such lofty principles as free trade, free seas, arms reduction, independence, self-determination of peoples, no annexations and an end to secret treaties. They were capped by Wilson's dearest dream: a League of Nations—a world government to arbitrate national disputes and put an end, once and forever, to war. Wilson, one of the greatest living scholars on government, was acutely aware of the urgent need for some kind of international machinery to preserve order.

Wilson's Fourteen Points made a crucial impact on Germany. After Germany's last five great offensives failed, when the suffering on the German home front became unbearable, after the German navy had mutinied, when Bolshevik revolutions threatened in Munich, Hamburg and Berlin, when Austria had collapsed completely and when the German armies were being pushed relentlessly back toward the Rhine, the shaky German Government remembered Wilson's Fourteen Points and, applying directly to him, asked for an armistice.

On November 11, 1918, nineteen months after America's entry, the ghastly war was over.

It had taken a terrible toll. America's 50,000 men killed and an additional 57,000 dead of disease (mostly from the influenza that swept the army camps at the end of the war) were a mere handful compared with the over-all soldier dead of thirteen million. An additional ten million civilians had died from famine and disease. The continent lay in poverty and ruins. An entire generation had been virtually wiped out. (The French military academy included in its long list of war dead the poignant entry: "The Class of 1914.")

Out of this terrible calamity grew the steely determination, *"Never again!"* The millions of lives must *not* have been sacrificed in vain. "Nothing but a new world is worth the price of the war" was the prevailing feeling.

With a deep sense of the enormity of his mission, Woodrow Wilson went to Europe to found this new world. He fully realized that his trip would be "either . . . the greatest success or the supremest tragedy in all history."

The suffering humanity of Europe met Wilson by the millions—crowds larger than anyone recalled ever having seen—their banners hailing him as "God of Peace," "Wilson the Just," "Crusader for Humanity." "No one ever had such cheers," reported a journalist. The French premier gasped, "I do not think there has been anything like it in the history of the world."

For six months Wilson labored to fulfill the people's expectations, even sacrificing his health (he probably suffered his first stroke during that time). The task was enormous. Never before had so many separate victors tried to concoct one peace treaty. And the issues were extremely complicated, with historical, geographical, economic, religious, military, political, cultural and nationalistic considerations. Even Wilson's Fourteen Points and supplementary ones failed him. In invoking one to unravel a snarl, he frequently violated another.

Many countries made huge demands. Some had already concluded secret treaties, parceling out the enemy's territory. Wilson, representing the only nation that asked for nothing, should have been the ideal person to arbitrate the claims and disputes, but perhaps the task was humanly impossible.

Besides, Wilson was no politician, accustomed to dealing with the possible. He was a visionary, and his talents lay in reaching for the stars. He had no taste for the irksome details on the ground. Nor could he view those details realistically. He saw them only in moral terms: good or evil, right or wrong. It was a grievous defect.

The other Allied leaders, meeting Wilson for the first time, were surprised to discover that he was not really a statesman; he was a schoolteacher, a stiff-necked "theocrat" who liked to lecture and preach. "We are going to have difficulties with this Presbyterian," grumbled Georges Clemenceau of France. The Allied leaders, according to Britain's Lloyd George, became increasingly "impatient at having little sermonettes delivered to them." Clemenceau finally cried in exasperation, "Woodrow Wilson bores me with his Fourteen Points. Why, God Almighty had only ten!"

Wilson successfully resisted the more outrageous Allied

demands, but the final product—the Treaty of Versailles—was a far cry from his ideal of "a peace without victory." Although it was undoubtedly kinder than what a victorious Germany would have imposed, it nevertheless saddled Germany with all guilt for the war, stripped her of her colonies, disarmed her and levied staggering reparations.

But it also created a League of Nations, and Wilson saw this as "the key to the whole settlement." He counted heavily upon this League to iron out the many wrinkles created in the "madhouse" confusion of the peace conference. In his intense concentration on this one answer, he lost contact with some of the realities. His greatest blind spot was with his own people. He didn't dream that they would ever, under any circumstances, reject membership in his League. This was crucial, for without the United States, now the world's most powerful nation, the League could not function effectively.

All in all, the Treaty of Versailles was a failure. The League was emasculated when the United States refused participation, and what was left contained the seeds for another war. The treaty was not as harsh as France had wanted it to be; nor was it gentle and supportive, as Wilson would have preferred. It was, rather, a compromise, carrying the weaknesses of both extremes while canceling out the strengths. The Treaty of Versailles neither built Germany up so that she could become a harmonious, self-respecting member of the world community nor destroyed her so completely that she could never wage war again. It left her dangerously embittered but essentially intact, with all her potential strength preserved.

"This is not peace," gasped France's horrified Marshal Ferdinand Foch. "It is an armistice for twenty years."

A vengeful Germany would rise again.

VIII

"Never Again!"

Now we come to one of the most painful chapters in world history: that in which a weary and wounded humanity, traumatized by a monstrous war, determined to its very depths that there would never be another and, in its very determination, made all the mistakes that brought forth an even more horrible one. Nothing more clearly demonstrates that sheer determination is not enough to avoid warfare.

Americans were naïve enough to believe that determination was all that was necessary, that there would be no more wars *"if mothers all would say, 'I didn't raise my boy to be a soldier!'"* They viewed peace negatively, as the absence of war and, therefore, a condition that would ensue automatically, without work or commitment. And they were particularly blind to any responsibility of their own in achieving or keeping peace.

This attitude was actually slow in developing. When President Woodrow Wilson returned from Paris in 1919 with the Treaty of Versailles and its provision for a League of Nations to keep the peace, the overwhelming majority of Americans were still filled with the crusading fervor of the war and a desire to make the world forever safe for democracy. They favored joining such a League of Nations. This was clearly seen from newspaper polls and the declarations of many interest groups, including chambers of commerce throughout the country. Thirty-two state legislatures passed resolutions supporting American membership in the League. "If we remain out of it," declared a former Supreme Court Justice, "war will come as the last one did, without our having any opportunity to prevent it and with only the privilege of fighting our way out of it."

Unfortunately, these views were not shared by the Republican-controlled U.S. Senate—that body whose two-thirds approval was required, by constitutional provision, on any foreign treaty. And Wilson's handling of the Senate on this matter was fatally inept.

Wilson had never had much use for Congressmen; he thought them "pygmy minded." He was especially suspicious of Republicans, whom he viewed as enemies. He liked to work alone. He had refused to take a Senator, or even a Republican of any stature, to the Peace Conference with him. While in Paris he failed to keep Congress adequately informed of his activities. The document that he signed at Versailles, in the name of all America, was not even available for Congressional perusal until it had become a *fait accompli*.

When Wilson returned home, he was too exhausted from his labors to present the treaty tactfully. He irritated many

Republican Senators (who were by now furious anyway) with a seemingly arrogant attitude, as if he were saying, "*I've* remade the world. You've no right to question what *I've* done. Just okay it."

Wilson contemptuously dismissed all honest opposition as "wrong." He did not understand that many of the Senators who opposed American membership in the League were sincere. "If I have had a conviction throughout my life with which it has been possible for me to be consistent at all times," declared Senator William Borah of Idaho, "it has been the conviction that we should stay out of European and Asiatic affairs."

However obsolete such views may have been, they were nevertheless heartfelt, and Wilson's intolerance of them was infuriating. Thus the great issue degenerated into a personality battle. The Chairman of the Senate Foreign Relations Committee, Henry Cabot Lodge, was especially motivated by an intense hatred of Wilson—a hatred which he repeatedly expressed in private and which Wilson, incidentally, returned in full measure.

Lodge's opposition was implacable: "I have ever had but one allegiance; I cannot divide it now. I have loved but one flag, and I cannot share that devotion and give affection to the mongrel banner invented for a League. National I must remain. . . ."

Seeing the Senate as hopelessly recalcitrant, Wilson took the issue directly to the people. He set out on a grueling cross-country speaking tour. He was exhausted from his work in Paris ("I'm at the end of my tether," he confided to his secretary) and plagued with blinding headaches, but "I cannot put my personal safety in the balance against my duty." The

League of Nations could not function effectively without American participation, and if the League failed, "I hate to think of what will happen to the world."

He traveled 8,000 miles in less than a month, delivering thirty-six major speeches and countless rear-platform talks. The turnouts were enormous, the crowds roaringly enthusiastic. Everyone seemed to understand Wilson's insistence that "this nation went into this war to see it through to the end, and the end has not yet come."

"See how the whole world turns with outstetched hands to this blessed country of ours, and says, 'If you lead, we will follow,'" Wilson cried dramatically. "God helping us, we will lead! . . . Dare we reject this treaty and break the heart of the world?"

If America dared, "I can predict with absolute certainty that within another generation there will be another world war . . ." and one that could not be compared with "the war we have just been through, though it was shot through with terror. . . . What the Germans used were toys compared to what would be used in the next war."

In Pueblo, Colorado, he became unusually emotional: "What of our pledges to the men that lie dead in France?" He lost his train of thought and tears streamed down his cheeks as he talked of "those dear ghosts."

Something was obviously wrong. That night he could hardly speak. "His face was pale and wan," reported his secretary. "One side of it had fallen, and his condition was indeed pitiful to behold." He was rushed back to Washington.

Shortly thereafter he suffered a massive cerebral thrombosis; his left side was paralyzed. For weeks he hung precariously close to death. He never really recovered.

The tragedy became complete when his wife, his secretary and his doctor—motivated by misguided devotion—shrouded his illness in secrecy. No one was permitted to see him. The wildest rumors abounded: Wilson was dead, insane, a prisoner. "If you would just tell the people exactly what is the matter with the President," one Cabinet member implored Wilson's doctor, "a wave of sympathy would pour in." But the people were told nothing.

They could not sustain Wilson's idealism without him. He had always been too far ahead of them. Without his continual inspiration, they lost all interest in his exhausting crusade. They wanted only to return to "normalcy."

A sick and disabled Wilson ("If only I were not helpless"), his judgment seriously impaired, could do no more than adamantly refuse to compromise with Senate leaders who urged limited membership in the League ("Let Lodge compromise"). The final vote—seven short of the required two-thirds—rejected American participation in the League of Nations.

Thus the United States "broke the heart of the world," renouncing the attempt of its own president to substitute legal machinery for the ancient horror of war. "The people of America have repudiated a fruitful leadership for a barren independence," Wilson said sadly. ". . . We had a chance to gain the leadership of the world. We have lost it, and soon we shall be witnessing the tragedy of it all."

If America had joined the League of Nations, would there have been a second world war? Who knows? Even today, when the world is far wiser, the United Nations is sadly incapable of handling serious disputes. A world government without real power is little better than no government at all.

Still, the effort should have been made. Without the United States, the League was doomed before it started.

But the mistakes that went into the making of World War II were many, and the failure of the League was only one of them. World War II occurred because a man named Adolph Hitler rose to power in Germany, and because, once he was launched on his deadly course, no one dared to stop him. Hitler was encouraged and buttressed by totalitarian regimes in Italy and Japan, but he was the key figure. Without his evil genius there would possibly never have been a second world war.

The groundwork for Hitler's spectacular rise was laid during World War I. We know now that the first seeds were sown in November, 1917, when the Bolsheviks seized control of Russia's new representative government. Such a takeover could never have occurred under normal conditions; it was a direct consequence of the war's horror and a prime example of how one war can breed another.

Bolshevism was an extreme movement. It contained all the evils of tyranny, including an inclination for violence and a brutal suppression of all opposition; moreover, it was frankly revolutionary, threatening existing social and economic structures. It spread terror throughout much of the world.

The triumph of any extreme is dangerous, for it weakens the forces of moderation and invites polarization. Thus the triumph of bolshevism encouraged the triumph of an opposing extreme: fascism.

Fascism first appeared in Italy, a country that had suffered greatly during the war and was experiencing much postwar disorder. A Bolshevist, or Communist, takeover of Italy appeared likely. Then fascism gathered force under the dynamic leadership of Benito Mussolini. Embracing mostly young war veterans and supported by wealthy businessmen, it advocated "order, hierarchy, discipline." In 1922 Mussolini's black-shirted followers staged a dramatic march on Rome and seized control, of the government. Once in power, Mussolini stamped out communism. He crushed the labor unions, banned strikes and protests, regimented the schools and the press and purged all opposition through a terroristic secret police.

When Italy quieted down under his iron rule, conservatives throughout the world were impressed. "He made the trains run on time" was a frequent compliment. Even in the United States some people were saying, "What this country needs is a Mussolini."

But Mussolini wanted far more than trains that ran on time. He wanted to "make a mark on my era with my will, like a lion with its claw!" Like many Italians, he believed that Italy had been short-changed at Versailles. He wanted what he thought Wilson ("that man from across the Atlantic with his hard jaw . . . and flat feet, full of false words and false teeth") had denied his country: territory—a little bit of the glory that once was Rome.

In Japan, the fear of communism likewise encouraged the growth of fascist groups. Many secret societies flourished, of which the fanatical Black Dragon was the most notorious. Openly committed to violence, they advocated a dictatorship by the army and envisioned Japanese control of the entire Far East—*Hakko Ichio,* "the eight corners of the world under one roof."

In Germany, Adolph Hitler rode to power on the fear of communism. At the critical moment he was supported by strong conservative groups who viewed him as a preferable alternative. Thus in their fear of bolshevism, many people failed to see the equally great danger of fascism. Too few grasped the fact that Hitler's spurs were the deadly ones of hatred and revenge, and that he would turn his anger not only on the communists but on *everyone.*

He roused his people with an almost hysterical appeal to their prejudices and embittered emotions. Thirsting for revenge and proof of superiority, he told the Germans that they were "the highest species of humanity on this earth." They had lost the Great War only because they had been betrayed by the "November criminals"—most particularly, the Socialists and the Jews. Hitler would know "neither rest nor peace until . . . on the ruins of a wretched Germany of today there should have arisen once more a Germany of power and greatness, of freedom and splendor." He would free the German people from "the death sentence of Versailles." He would lead them to victory, ushering in "a new millenium. . . ." "Today we rule Germany, tomorrow the world!"

To understand how acutely Hitler struck a German nerve, we need only return to World War I. The Germans, after all, had seen that conflict as a righteous one of self-defense. Like the British and the French, they had simply fought for their country. (Even Woodrow Wilson, early in the war, had felt that their goals of all the warring nations were "the same.")

When the German army was broken on the battlefield in 1918, the German Government agreed to an armistice on the basis of Wilson's Fourteen Points. They expected generous treatment.

Many people in the Allied countries opposed this armistice. They thought that Germany should be invaded and the German people brought to their knees once and for all. Ex-President Theodore Roosevelt wanted to "dictate peace by the hammering guns" rather than by "the clicking of typewriters." But President Wilson felt that it would be morally wrong to reject any opportunity to end the frightful bloodletting.

Unfortunately, the Allied military leaders did not realize how desperate German's situation actually was. Had they known, they could have imposed suitably stern armistice terms and the Germans would have known exactly where they stood. Instead, the severe measures were deferred to the final treaty, and in the moment of victory an impulsive magnanimity reigned. "They fought well," Marshal Ferdinand Foch reasoned. "Let them keep their weapons." And so the German soldiers marched home with their rifles over their shoulders.

The German people received them as conquering heroes. They had too much pride in their glorious army to grasp the shattering truth—that they had been beaten on the battlefield and had lost a war—especially since such a contretemps was not clearly demonstrated to them. Many convinced themselves that the Allies had finally recognized the existence of a hopeless stalemate and had agreed to negotiate a peace, virtually between equals.

Thus the Treaty of Versailles was a cruel shock. Not that it was unduly harsh or unjust—the treaty which the Germans had imposed upon the defeated Russians at Brest-Litovsk only one year earlier had been shockingly more severe—but because the Germans did not see themselves as vanquished. Now they saw themselves as betrayed—not only by the Allies but by their own leaders, those whom Hitler would repeatedly call the "November criminals."

This gigantic myth—that the Germans had not lost the war on the battlefield but had been "betrayed"—was the germ that sprouted into another war. Seized on by the demented Hitler, it provided the goad for conquest—a determination to prove once and for all the superiority of the humiliated German nation.

The greatest hope for peace lay in the success of Germany's new democratic government, the Weimar Republic, but never was a regime launched under such a stigma: it had to sign the hated Treaty of Versailles, war guilt clause and all. ("May the hand wither that signs such a peace!" one indignant German leader had cried, but the Government had no choice.)

The early years of the Republic were not very promising. Germany, already burdened with her own war debts, had been stripped by her victors of all of her colonies and some of her best farmlands and deprived for at least fifteen years of the riches of her own Saar Valley, and she was now saddled with reparations that exceeded all reason. When she failed to meet her heavy reparation payments, French troops occupied her chief industrial areas and seized her coal reserves. German factories ground to a halt. Unemployment spread like wildfire. The Weimar Government in desperation began printing money for which it had no credit. A rampant inflation ensued. Barrels of marks were soon required to buy a loaf of bread. Most middle-class families were ruined. Rioting erupted in the streets. Two of the nation's leaders were assassinated.

The Weimar Government actually survived this disaster, thanks to huge loans from American businessmen, who felt that it was in their own interests to build Germany into a healthy customer. But then came the reckoning: October, 1929, and the crash of the American stock market.

Since New York was the financial center of the world, the effects spread throughout the globe. The American crash provoked eleven revolutions in Latin America alone. It precipi-

tated a world run on Germany, as financiers frantically attempted to salvage $6 billion worth of investments. The
desperate conditions that resulted were fatal. They dealt the
finishing blow to the hated Weimar Republic and opened the
doors to the insane leadership of Adolph Hitler.

The American people journeyed through those years happily
oblivious to any connection between their own actions and
events abroad. They had no interest in the rest of the world.
The Great War had begun in Europe, they reasoned, so let's
turn our backs on Europe and mind our own business and
never get involved again—as if the war had not clearly shown
that they, as citizens of a major power, could no longer escape
the consequences of events abroad. Americans reverted blindly
to their traditional pattern of isolation, initiated almost 150
years earlier, when their country was young and weak.

But in 1920 the United States, having emerged the only
undamaged victor of a terrible war, was the richest nation
on earth. Its agriculture and industry, which had expanded
enormously to meet the war's needs, were feeding and rebuild-
ing Europe. America was producing nearly 40 per cent of the
world's pig iron, almost 40 per cent of the world's coal and
nearly 70 per cent of all crude petroleum. Branches of her
business corporations encircled the globe, directly affecting
many far-flung areas. American overseas investments were
enormous. Americans controlled so much of the world's production, trade and capital that other governments could not
act without closely watching the United States. As Woodrow
Wilson had so carefully explained, "The isolation of the United
States is at an end not because we chose to go into the politics
of the world . . . but because we have become a determining
factor in the history of mankind." The Europe that had once

policed the world was broken and in ruins. There was only one power that could take its place. "The other countries of the world," Woodrow Wilson had insisted, "are looking to us for leadership and direction."

They got nothing. During the 1920s American leadership was unusually poor. Warren G. Harding, who succeeded Wilson as president, was, in his own words, "a man of limited talents from a small town." He did not "know anything about this European stuff." Nor could he "make a damn thing out of this tax problem. . . . I know somewhere there is a book that will give me the truth; but hell! I couldn't read the book."

Harding's successor, "Silent Cal" Coolidge, never took the reins. He thought that a president should "interfere" as little as possible. "He knew nothing and refused to learn," according to one of his biographers. His chief feat, according to H. L. Mencken, "was to sleep more than any other President." When asked how he stayed fit in a job that had broken the health of Woodrow Wilson, Coolidge explained, "By avoiding the big problems." He avoided them so assiduously that he was reduced to filling in his empty hours rocking on the front porch of the White House. When Secret Service men expressed alarm, Coolidge insisted that he wanted to "be out here where I can see the streetcars go by."

While Coolidge rocked and watched the streetcars, his country led the world to disaster. The Great Depression of 1930, which played a vital role in the rise of Adolph Hitler, was an American product. Economists disagree over the deep-seated causes of the Depression, but all recognize, among other things, America's tariff and war-debt policies as vital factors.

These policies were patently foolish. Americans insisted on collecting their war debts from the Allied countries while erecting the highest tariff barriers in their history. Obviously those tariffs prevented the Allies from selling their products in the United States. Denied this important market, they had great trouble paying their debts.

Many Europeans felt that Americans should have regarded money lent during the war as a contribution to the common cause. They felt that a sacrifice of American dollars (especially since those dollars had been spent on American products) could not be compared with the enormous human losses incurred by the Europeans. Europe had borne the burden of the war, and now it was being asked to toil, perhaps for centuries, to make "Uncle Shylock" richer while it remained hopelessly poor.

Economists tried to point out that the transmission of such large sums of cash by countries that could ill afford to pay was dangerous, but President Coolidge could not see it. "They hired the money, didn't they?" he reasoned. "Let them repay it." The U.S. Congress angrily resolved that it was against its policy "that any of the indebtedness of foreign countries to the United States should be in any manner canceled or reduced." When Congress at the same time debated raising American tariff walls even higher, 1,000 economic experts (and, as one historian has pointed out, 1,000 economists seldom agree on anything) signed a strong protest, but Herbert Hoover, who was then president, ignored the protest, and up went the tariff walls. The result was a severe stagnation of world trade, the depletion of European gold reserves and a general undermining of world currencies.

Yet Americans continued to give full lip service to the cause of peace! It became an article of faith that they would never go to war again. To ensure this, they helped negotiate treaty after treaty—none of which contained any provision for enforcement. Mere words, Americans hoped, could be a happy substitute for responsible commitment.

Disarmament was obviously a first step. Here the lesson of the Great War appeared clear: a rampant arms race, such as Europe had experienced before 1914, was bound to eventually result in war. The answer seemed so simple: If nations would refuse to prepare for war, then there would be no war. The catch—that disarmament was effective only if *all* nations disarmed—did not trouble most people. "The only way to disarm," announced Harding's Secretary of State, "is to disarm."

President Harding called a disarmament conference in Washington, which resulted in several treaties that were widely acclaimed—especially since those treaties, as the President happily pointed out, did not commit the United States "to any kind of alliance, entanglement or involvement." When wiser heads pointed out that the treaties did not commit anyone to anything, the President replied, "Let us accept no such doctrine of despair as that."

Certainly the United States intended to do its part. It energetically disarmed—sinking, scrapping and demilitarizing thousands of tons of war vessels until the U.S. Navy was even smaller than the treaties stipulated. "Schools not Battleships" was a popular slogan. Americans scrupulously honored their agreement not to fortify their Pacific possessions (the ambitious Japanese were not so conscientious), and disbanded their army.

If they needed further assurance that they would never go to war again, they received it in 1928 when their Secretary of State, Frank B. Kellogg, engineered the Kellogg-Briand Pact, outlawing war forever. "A brilliant achievement," cried newspaper editorials. Sixty-two nations—including Germany, Italy and Japan—promised to forgo war "as an instrument of national policy." The dream of peace on earth had at long last been realized!

Americans continued working enthusiastically for peace even after this "great accomplishment." Throughout the 1920s and the 1930s they wrote, marched and demonstrated. Such organizations as the National Conference on the Cause and Cure of War and the Emergency Peace Campaign thrived. Ladies' clubs protested the manufacturing of toy soldiers, and some even suggested abolishing Memorial Day. Pacifist broadsides flooded the country portraying such scenes as a veteran in a wheel chair with the tasteless caption *"Hello, Sucker."* In Great Britain, the undergraduates of Oxford University resolved "never to fight for King and country," and this historic "Oxford Pledge" swept American campuses. The literature of the period was heavily antiwar, with the horrors of the 1914-18 conflict so graphically portrayed that any lingering romantic illusions were forever dispelled. "What is there so dear that it is worth dying for?" asked a character in Irwin Shaw's *Bury the Dead.* "Very few things," was the reply, "and never the things for which one nation fights another."

A massive reaction against the Great War set in. Americans began to feel that they had been duped, taken in by flags and parades—that indeed they need not have entered that conflict at all. Revisionist historians proffered the view that the United States had been dragged into the war by its munitions makers, those "merchants of death"—although, in fact, American industrialists had been as horrified by the war as anyone else. (Besides, they had had nothing to gain by entering it, since they were already enjoying its profits without any of its sacrifices.) Another popular theory was that Americans had fallen prey to Allied propaganda. To an extent this was true. Americans had been unusually receptive to Allied propaganda from the very beginning, for many reasons, but in the end it was not so much what anyone said as what Germany did that had finally forced America's hand.

Still, anti-German propaganda had whipped the people into such a frenzy of hatred that a reaction had to come. People were bound to realize, sooner or later, that Germans were human beings. Such literary masterpieces as Erich Maria Remarque's *All Quiet on the Western Front* shocked the Western world into a realization that the German soldiers had been just like their own. Americans and many West Europeans came to feel that no one could be viewed as "bad" or an "enemy." But, alas, their new sophistication was ill-timed. Indeed, it seems the cruelest irony of all that when people were finally learning the valuable lesson of tolerance, along came Adolph Hitler.

Thus did good intentions, shorn of wisdom, lead to calamity. Americans sought not to become "involved," yet their very existence implicated them intricately in every aspect of world affairs. When they determined to go their own way without regard of others, their selfishness hurt everyone. When they learned not to view anyone as "evil," along came one of the most evil men in the history of the world. When this man needed to be crushed, people strove to "understand" him. When the only hope of stopping him lay in sheer military might, Americans avidly disarmed and swore never to fight again. They had to learn the hard way the fruitlessness of vowing "Never again!" when anyone anywhere was screaming "Again!"

"Again" was what the poor world got—and many times over.

IX

World War II

September 18, 1931 . . . the Japanese Army invaded Chinese Manchuria.

The Japanese Government was astonished. It had had no foreknowledge of this event. The army was starting to run amok, and the Government was soon powerless to control it.

The army was motivated by its dreams of a great Japanese empire—dreams inherent in Japan's coming of age. In order to understand, one need only remember how Americans felt before the Spanish-American War. A nation that has "arrived" experiences an enormous desire to flex its muscles. It longs for recognition.

In Japan's case, these longings were intensified by the Western world's repeated frustration of them—after Japan's victory over China in 1895, after her victory over Russia ten years

160

later; when it squelched Japan's outrageous Twenty-One Demands of China in 1915 and even at Versailles, where it com-
promised Japan's hopes of gaining all of Germany's Far
Eastern possessions and refused to incorporate a racial equality
clause into the Covenant of the League of Nations. This last
defeat was a particularly galling blow to Japanese pride,
following as it did many discriminatory acts against Japanese
in the state of California. Subsequent American immigration
laws which excluded all Asians from the United States did not
help; and the Washington naval limitations treaty giving Japan
the short end of a 5:5:3 battleship ratio was also seen as an
insult—further proof that the world did not recognize Japan
as a major power.

These setbacks were grist for the militarists' mills. By the
time the Japanese Army moved into Manchuria in 1931, it
had acquired a considerable political following. It proceeded
to consolidate its power by completing its conquest of Manchuria and assassinating civilian opponents at home, including
the premier. Fanatical leaders even considered murdering U.S.
Ambassador Joseph Grew and actor Charlie Chaplin, who
was then visiting Tokyo, in the hopes of provoking a war with
the United States, and thereby assuring military control of
the government.

China, aghast at the invasion of Manchuria, appealed to the
League of Nations. The League requested Japan to withdraw
her forces pending an investigation. When Japan ignored the
request, a real crisis was at hand.

Great Britain and France sounded out the U.S. Government.
Would it cooperate if the League applied sanctions against
Japan? No, it would not. President Herbert Hoover adamantly
opposed the use of sanctions, "either economic or military, for

those are the roads to war." The American people whole-
heartedly supported him. They had no wish to get involved.

Because of America's economic power, sanctions without her
cooperation were meaningless. So the League did nothing
as Japan set up the puppet state of Manchukuo, annexed the
adjacent Chinese province of Jehol and then marched troops
to the Great Wall.

The lesson was clear for all the world to see: The League
was a paper tiger; an aggressor nation could move without
interference.

March 10, 1935 . . . Adolf Hitler, who had been secretly
rearming Germany, boldly announced the existence of a German air force. Six days later he decreed compulsory military
service and spoke frankly of a German army—all blatant violations of the Treaty of Versailles and a direct challenge to the
League of Nations.

The League issued a strong protest, signed by nineteen
countries, but did not act. Germany was now free to openly
and feverishly prepare for war.

Of all the countries in Europe, perhaps the most alarmed
was France. Three times in a hundred years the Prussian
hordes had crossed her borders. "My house was in the hands
of the Germans in 1814, again in 1870 and again in 1914,"
Clemenceau had said at Versailles. "I pray God that He will
make it impossible that it shall ever be in their hands again."

But France was torn by internal dissension; the Great War
had left her physically and spiritually drained. She lacked the
courage to act without full support from Britain.

And Britain was overrun with pacifist sentiment. The prevailing British view was that the Treaty of Versailles had

been unjust; why not let Hitler correct it, especially since he was, after all, an opponent of communism? There was also a tragic tendency to misread the lessons of the Great War. That war had come after a frantic arms race; therefore, Great Britain would not arm. That war had affected the entire continent because every major power had been committed to aid another; therefore, Great Britain would not commit herself to anyone.

Across the Atlantic, the American ostrich reacted by digging her head deeper into the sand, disregarding Woodrow Wilson's 1919 admonitions that the only way to prevent American participation in another world war was to prevent such a war from ever occurring. "To hell with Europe and the rest of those nations!" cried a Senator on the floor of Congress. Congress, still mired mentally back in 1917, passed a series of neutrality acts prohibiting the sale of munitions to any belligerent country. Thus the United States sought to save its own skin by withdrawing behind its ocean ramparts and leaving the world to Hitler.

October 3, 1935 . . . Italy's Benito Mussolini invaded the ancient mountain kingdom of Ethiopia, one of the last independent states in Africa. His excuse for this startling act was the *withdrawal* of Ethiopian soldiers from their own border, a "strategic move" which "necessitated" an immediate advance into the country to protect Italy's neighboring colonies!

The League of Nations promptly declared Italy an aggressor and invoked sanctions in the form of arms, credit and raw-material embargoes, *but not oil,* Italy's greatest foreign need.

These limited sanctions, timidly enforced, had no effect, while America's contribution—denying military aid to both

sides in accordance with her neutrality laws—hurt only unarmed Ethiopia.

In May, 1936, after seven months of fighting, Italian troops
entered the capital city of Addis Ababa, and Mussolini formally
annexed the little country. The lesson Japan had learned in
Manchuria was clearly confirmed.

March 7, 1936 . . . in a surprise move at dawn, three small
German battalions crossed the bridges over the Rhine River
and occupied the neutral demilitarized Rhineland. This was
a shockingly bold act, defying both the Treaty of Versailles
and the 1925 Locarno Agreements with France.

At Versailles, France had been almost paranoic about de-
manding a buffer zone between herself and her terrifying
neighbor. Now that the German army had in one fell swoop
erased such a zone, what would France do?

The German military command was scared. The French
had thirteen divisions concentrated near the German border.
"Considering the situation we were in," German General Al-
fred Jodl testified ten years later at Nuremberg, "the French
covering army could have blown us to pieces." The German
soldiers had explicit orders to beat a hasty retreat if the French
made a move.

"The forty-eight hours after the march into the Rhineland
were the most nerve-racking in my life," Hitler later confessed. "If the French had then marched . . . we would have
had to withdraw with our tails between our legs." Hitler
knew that his political career might never have survived such
a fiasco.

But again, France would not act without Britain, and Britain shied away from the risk of war. "The Germans, after

all, are only going into their own back garden," they reasoned.

Britain and France, having lost their last chance of stopping Hitler short of war, took heart from his promise: "We have no territorial demands to make in Europe! . . . Germany will never break the peace!"

July 17, 1936 . . . bloody civil war broke out in Spain when army officials revolted against their leftist government. The world soon witnessed a terrifying preview of its own fate as Spain became the testing ground for the weapons and tactics of World War II. Hitler and Mussolini sent enormous aid to the insurgent leader, General Francisco Franco. German and Italian planes, perfecting their techniques of aerial bombardment, converted cities to rubble, killing civilians by the thousands.

The United States gasped at this gory dress rehearsal. Congress stiffened its neutrality laws, forbidding Americans to travel on belligerent ships and permitting nonmilitary trade on a cash-and-carry basis only, thus readily surrendering the "neutral rights" and "freedom of the seas" which Woodrow Wilson had deemed so important.

Never was a nation more terrified of being drawn into a war; never was one more determined to remain at peace.

July 7, 1937 . . . fighting broke out between Japanese forces and a Chinese garrison near the Marco Polo Bridge not far from Peiping. Hostilities quickly spread, and a full-scale war was soon in progress.

Shocked by these events, the American president, Franklin D. Roosevelt, dramatically urged his people to face reality. International order had broken down, he said, and an "epidemic of world lawlessness" was spreading. "When an epidemic of physical disease starts to spread, the community joins in a quarantine of the patients in order to protect the health of the community against the spread of the disease." The "peace-loving nations must make a concerted effort" to protect the peace. No nation could "isolate itself from what goes on in the rest of the world." He sternly warned: "Let no one imagine that America will escape, that America may expect mercy, that this Western Hemisphere will not be attacked."

This famous "Quarantine Speech" provoked a barrage of criticism. Many people felt that Roosevelt was "saber-rattling," that he was trying to embroil his country in "foreign wars." Several Republican Congressmen sensed the forbidden specter of "entangling alliances" in Roosevelt's talk of a "concerted effort," and all the old emotions over membership in the League of Nations were aroused. There was angry talk of impeaching the President.

In the meantime, the Japanese moved up the Yangtze River to capture the capital city of Nanking, where they shocked the world by turning their soldiers loose upon the helpless civilian populace. Then they seized Soochow, Amoy, Hankow and Canton, and finally occupied the entire eastern seaboard.

In the war that continued to rage throughout the rest of China, Japanese airplanes deliberately bombed American missionary churches, hospitals and schools. According to the Chinese, the most dangerous spot in an air raid was an American institution. During the next few years the U.S. Government vigorously protested over two hundred such incidents, including the sinking of the American gunboat *Panay* on the Yangtze River and the deliberate strafing of its survivors.

March 13, 1938 . . . German troops marched into Austria. With local Nazis, who had performed the undercover work, they seized Vienna. Hitler announced the annexation of the entire country.

September 26, 1938 . . . Adolf Hitler, in a ranting speech, demanded the German-populated Sudentenland from Czechoslovakia. "This is the last territorial claim I have to make in Europe," he insisted. He had secretly set October 1 as the invasion date.

The Czechs had no intention of yielding this territory. They mobilized for war. Their army consisted of thirty-five divisions—one and one-half million well-armed, well-trained men. Their air force was one of the best in the world. Their fortifications high on the Bohemian escarpments were, in the opinion of the leading German generals, invincible. "We did not have the means to break through," several of them testified after the war.

Soviet Premier Josef Stalin, horrified by a German move in his direction, sought commitments from Britain and France to join him in defending Czechoslovakia. He sensed that Germany was not yet prepared to wage a two-front war. Indeed, the German generals were so convinced that such a feat was "militarily impossible" at that time that they were planning a coup against Hitler, if necessary, to avert the disaster.

But the fear of communism precluded any cooperation with Russia. And while France seriously considered supporting Czechoslovakia, again she would not act without Britain, and the last thing Britain wanted was another war. Her prime minister, Neville Chamberlain, was determined upon peace at any price. He made arrangements to meet with Hitler.

"Ich bin vom Himmel gefallen!" ("I am fallen from Heaven!") Hitler exclaimed in happy astonishment. He had never dared hope, in his wildest moments, that the head of the mighty British Empire would come personally begging favors from him.

History, with the knowledge of hindsight, has cruelly condemned Neville Chamberlain for his appeasement of Hitler. Actually the foolish Chamberlain was merely a product of his time. In 1938, his efforts were widely acclaimed. If only the British had attempted this sort of sensible negotiation in 1914, people felt, the Great War might have been avoided! "It seems to me that the Prime Minister of England did a fine thing when he went to visit the German Chancellor in a last effort to prevent bloodshed," Mrs. Franklin Roosevelt wrote in her daily newspaper column. "It seems insanity . . . to try to settle the difficult problems of today by the unsatisfactory method of going to war." Few could see that by that time war was the only answer.

Chamberlain met with Hitler three times—the last at Munich on September 29, when France's Premier Edouard Daladier was also present. An anxious Czech delegation waited outside, buttonholing one of Chamberlain's aides for information when he briefly emerged.

"You are sacrificing our defenses!" the Czechs tried to tell him. Frantically they spread out a map. "Look, this is our defensive line—and here—and here—and here. All given to the Nazis!"

"I am sorry," Chamberlain's aide replied irritably. "It is no use arguing. I have no time to listen. I must go back in."

Inside, a miserable Daladier and a yawning Chamberlain gave a triumphant Hitler 11,000 square miles containing 66 per cent of Czechoslovakia's coal, 80 per cent of her lignite, 70 per cent of her iron and steel, 80 per cent of her cement and textiles, 40 per cent of her timber, 76 per cent of her railway carriage works, 70 per cent of her electrical power supplies and 86 per cent of her glass and chemicals.

Daladier returned to France overcome with "a great bitterness" at this betrayal of "a faithful ally" (Czechoslovakia). To his surprise, his people, immeasurably relieved that a threatened war had been averted, gave him a hero's welcome. Half a million wildly cheering Frenchmen lined his route from the airport into Paris. "The imbeciles," Daladier commented to an aide—"if they only knew what they were acclaiming."

Neville Chamberlain also landed in triumph. "No conqueror returning from a victory on the battlefield has come adorned with nobler laurels," declared the London *Times*. To a great crowd that met him at the airport singing *"For He's a Jolly Good Fellow!"* Chamberlain happily reported that he had achieved "peace! peace with honor . . . peace in our time!"

One of the few Englishmen to criticize Chamberlain's actions was former Cabinet member Winston Churchill. "We have sustained a total and unmitigated defeat," he told the House of Commons. Such a roar of protest broke out that he had to wait several minutes before he could resume speaking. No one wanted to hear the truth, which Churchill summed up neatly:

"Britain and France had to choose between war and dishonor. They chose dishonor. They will have war."

March 15, 1939 . . . Adolph Hitler, who had promised to stop with the Sudetenland, sent German troops marching into a fatally dismembered Czechoslovakia. They seized the capital city of Prague and occupied the entire country—their first conquest of a non-German-speaking people. "Czechoslovakia has ceased to exist," Hitler jubilantly announced.

Prime Minister Neville Chamberlain was speechless. At long last he realized the true nature of the man he had trusted at Munich.

One look at the map showed Chamberlain that Hitler's next victim would almost certainly be Poland. Among other things, Poland's corridor to the sea, awarded her at Versailles, had severed East Prussia from Germany, and Hitler obviously was not going to continue tolerating that.

Chamberlain finally offered trembling France the support she had long been seeking, and together Great Britain and France gave Hitler notice: if he attacked Poland, they would fight. Said Winston Churchill, echoing Woodrow Wilson: "God helping, we can do no other."

But alas, Hitler had no respect for the backbone of the British and French leaders. "They are little worms," he said. "I saw them at Munich."

He could not fathom that those two countries, having repeatedly refused to stop him when they could, would exert themselves when he was far more powerful and better situated. Especially in view of his next accomplishment.

August 23, 1939 . . . Hitler astounded the world by concluding a ten-year nonaggression pact with his most implacable ideological foe: the Soviet Union. Hitler did not dare invade Poland without first neutralizing Russia, and it was his fantastic luck to find Stalin receptive—a desperation move on the part of Stalin, who had failed in all his overtures to Britain and France.

Hitler offered excellent bait: half of Poland and a free hand in eastern Rumania, Finland and the Baltic states. The cunning Stalin accepted.

Dawn, September 1, 1939 . . . fifty-six German divisions crashed into Poland. Furious fighting ensued, but Russian troops poured in from the east and Poland was quickly crushed. After two agonizing days of diplomacy and ultimatums, a much shaken Britain and France made good their promises and declared war on Germany. World War II—so long dreaded, so avidly avoided—had begun.

Americans were aghast. Desperately they hoped that they could stay out of this new horror. But their sense of doom deepened as the news from abroad grew ever worse.

In the spring of 1940, Hitler launched "the most fearful military explosion so far known to man" (Churchill's words) —a *blitzkrieg* that took by storm the countries of Denmark, Norway, the Netherlands, Belgium, Luxembourg and (nobody could believe it) great and powerful France, sweeping to the sea with a savagery that rivaled the most terrible barbarism of old.

This massive, lightning conquest of Europe shocked many Americans into a hard look at their own defenses. So completely had they disarmed that they were by then, according to General Dwight Eisenhower, militarily "as close to zero as a great nation could conceivably be." The pathetic little Polish army, outnumbered three to one by the Germans and quickly obliterated, was far larger and better equipped than America's, while the U.S. Navy had only been raised to *disarmament* strength in 1938.

President Roosevelt pleaded for appropriations to build a

defense force, but progress was painfully slow. Pressure groups composed mainly of women and students crying for "peace" vigorously opposed every step. Like so many people throughout time immemorial, they could not change their views to meet a new situation.

"There is a race on between education and catastrophe, with catastrophe in the lead," said H. G. Welles.

"We have seen nation after nation go down, one after the other in front of a concentrated effort, each one lulled . . . into negative action, until all the guns were turned on them and it was too late," General George Marshall told Congress. "I do emphatically believe that the safety of this country is imperiled."

"I feel more up against it than ever before," Secretary of War Henry Stimson wrote in his diary. "It is a problem whether this country has it in itself to meet an emergency."

When President Roosevelt asked for a draft to raise an army, mothers dressed in mourning staged a death watch at the Capitol. "Give Our Sons Jobs Not Guns!" proclaimed their signs. Congress nevertheless authorized the first peacetime conscription in American history, and in October, 1940, the first numbers were drawn. The following August—only four months before Pearl Harbor—the bill to continue this draft raised another hornet's nest. It passed the House of Representatives by only one vote.

During all this time Great Britain was facing Nazi Germany alone. Americans watched, their hearts in their throats, as Nazi planes tried to blast England into submission. In those dark days, when no one seemed able to stop Hitler, they thrilled to the words of Britain's new prime minister, Winston Churchill: ". . . We shall defend our island, whatever the cost may be; we shall fight on the beaches, we shall fight on the landing-grounds, we shall fight in the fields and in the streets, we shall fight in the hills; we shall never surrender!"

Never before, not even during World War I, were Americans so completely united in their sympathies. Yet they disagreed bitterly over what to do about it. Many thought that they could avoid war by minding their own business and letting the chips fall willy-nilly in Europe. Others insisted that America's security depended on a British victory, which was patently impossible without American aid.

They pointed out that America's neutrality laws were helping Hitler, with his colossal war machine, by denying aid to virtually unarmed Great Britain. But when President Roosevelt urged Congress to lift the arms embargo and permit British purchases on a cash-and-carry basis, he provoked all those people who were still living back in 1917. "You will send munitions without pay and you will send your boys back to the slaughter pens of Europe!" cried Senator William Borah. Thousands of citizens urged their Congressmen to "keep America out of the blood business."

Congress, after two months of heated debate, passed the legislation. It sufficed until England ran out of "cash." Then President Roosevelt suggested a "lend-lease" program, in which aid could be sent without charge, to be repaid in kind, not dollars, sometime after the war. "Suppose my neighbor's home catches fire, and I have a length of garden hose," he told his countrymen. "If he can take my garden hose and connect it up with his hydrant, I may help him to put out his fire." It was senseless, he said, to quibble over who was going to pay for the hose; all that mattered was that the fire be put out. "What I am trying to do is eliminate the dollar sign."

"This is a bill for the destruction of the American republic," thought the Chicago *Tribune*. "The lend-lease-give
program . . . will plow under every fourth American boy,"
warned Senator Burton Wheeler. A mothers' crusade again
descended upon the Capitol, this time with signs urging
"Kill the Lend Lease Bill Not Our Boys."

But Roosevelt, while admitting that "there is risk in any
course we may take," insisted that "there is far less chance of
the United States getting into war, if we do all we can to
support the nations defending themselves against attack . . .
than if we acquiesce in their defeat . . . and wait our turn
to be the object of attack in another war later on."

The majority of Americans gradually became convinced
that they had no choice. England appeared to be *in extremis,*
and she was obviously all that stood between Nazi Germany
and America. "If we can stand up to him [Hitler], all Europe
may be free," Churchill had dramatically told his people. "But
if we fail, then the whole world, including the United States,
. . . will sink into the abyss of a new Dark Age, made more
sinister, and perhaps more protracted, by the lights of per-
verted science."

Hitler obviously had to be stopped, and Churchill's im-
passioned plea, "Give us the *tools* and we will finish the job!"
led Americans to hope against hope that the feat could be
accomplished through their manufactures, without the spilling
of American blood.

And so, on March 11, 1941, after months of heated debate,
Lend Lease became law. This was an act without parallel
in American history—the giving of "all aid short of war" to
a belligerent nation.

Thus America abandoned all pretense of neutrality and tried

to become the "arsenal of democracy." A steadily growing stream of planes, food, tanks, guns, ammunition and "supplies of all kinds" began to pour across the Atlantic.

As in World War I, German U-boats attacked this lifeline. As they ranged over the Atlantic, American ships were inevitably hit and American lives lost.

The freighter *Robin Moore* was sunk off the coast of Brazil. The destroyer *Greer* was attacked in the North Atlantic. The U.S.S. *Kearney* received a torpedo south of Iceland with the loss of eleven of her crew. And when the destroyer *Reuben James* went down 600 miles west of Iceland, 115 crewmen and every officer on board perished.

The sword of Damocles was hanging ever lower over the American people. At this stage of events in 1917 they had declared war.

President Roosevelt grimly addressed the nation: "When you see a rattlesnake poised to strike, you do not wait until he has struck before you crush him. These Nazi submarines and raiders are the rattlesnakes of the Atlantic. . . . Do not let us be hair-splitters. Let us not ask ourselves whether the Americas should begin to defend themselves after the first attack, or the fifth attack, or the tenth attack, or the twentieth attack. The time for active defense is now." Henceforth, American ships would shoot German vessels on sight. The United States was at undeclared naval war with Germany.

Like all great sagas, this one had its subplots, and while Hitler marched in Europe, a frightening sideshow took place in Asia.

As each European country went down, Japan began licking her chops over that country's Asiatic possessions. Most tempting were British Malaya and the Dutch East Indies—colonies opulent beyond imagination, rich in rubber, tin and oil. "Japan must with patience wait for the time of confusion in Europe to gain its objectives," a nineteenth-century Japanese statesman had advised. The time had obviously come. Europe's rich colonies appeared to be Japan's for the taking—except for one thing: directly between Japanese Formosa and the Dutch East Indies lay the American-owned Philippine Islands.

A more precarious location for an American possession could scarcely be imagined. Americans, dreaming of isolating themselves from an exploding world, could now regret having acquired such strategic territory 7,000 miles across the sea, but the Filipino people were nevertheless looking to them for protection.

In July, 1941, Japan swallowed all of French Indochina in one bloodless coup, effecting a horseshoe encirclement of the Philippines. President Roosevelt reacted immediately. He ceased all trade with Japan. This was drastic action, severing Japan from her main source of oil. It meant war, and Roosevelt knew it, but he felt that he had no honorable choice. America could not continue to feed Japan's military aggression.

Now the Japanese economy was in serious trouble. The Japanese would soon lack fuel oil for normal domestic use, not to mention the military operations so important to their ego. Now they desperately needed the great natural wealth of British Malaya and the Dutch East Indies.

Should they seize those lands, they would of course clash with the British and the free Dutch. But the Japanese saw America as their greatest obstacle. Not only did the Americans have a garrison in the Philippines, which could threaten their supply lines, but they also possessed a Pacific fleet, based in Hawaii. The Japanese felt that they could not move any further in Asia until they destroyed that fleet.

Japanese strategists began drafting plans for the greatest surprise assault in world history, detailing strikes against Pearl Harbor, Malaya, the Philippines, Hong Kong, north Borneo, Guam and Wake Island. The plans were outrageously ambitious, but with Germany diverting one-half of the world, Japan's chances for success in another corner appeared excellent.

The U.S. Government realized that war was inevitable. Its only goal, after July, was to stall for time—time to prod a snail-paced Congress for military appropriations, time to convert to full war production. The Japanese were willing to negotiate—for a while. If they did not attain their goals by the end of 1941, they would attack.

Negotiation was hopeless. The Japanese wanted American trade *and* a free hand in Asia. But the United States could not in all conscience resume trade until Japan ceased her aggression, pulled out of China and broke her alliance with Germany and Italy. There was no chance of this. Japan was too powerful, too far launched on the road of her dreams to turn back. Her navy was already stronger than the Pacific fleets of the United States, Great Britain and the free Netherlands combined.

November 3, 1941 . . . U.S. Ambassador Joseph Grew wired from Tokyo that Japan was preparing for war and might act "with dangerous and dramatic suddenness."

U.S. officials knew that Japan had started all of her three modern wars with surprise attacks—against China's fleet in

1894, against Russia's Pacific fleet at Port Arthur in 1904 and against the German stronghold in Shantung province in 1914. They expected just such a surprise attack, but when would it come and where? Most people thought it would be in the Philippines. There the tension, according to one general, "could be cut with a knife."

"It was like living near a neighbor who was big and burly and who you knew held a deadly grudge against you," the commander of the U.S. Asiatic Fleet later wrote. "You could see him building up his muscles and training himself to a fine edge for a fight. . . . You knew that sooner or later he was going to spring out of the darkness and slug you when you weren't looking. You knew that he would kill you if he could, but because you were peaceable and law-abiding you couldn't do much about it."

November 20, 1941 . . . the Japanese envoys in Washington handed Secretary of State Cordell Hull their last proposal. It so completely rejected American demands that Hull flatly announced that the issue was "no longer diplomatic." He warned the Secretaries of War and Navy to take care that the Japanese did not "stampede the hell out of our scattered forces" in the Pacific.

War warnings began radiating out of Washington: "HOSTILE ACTION POSSIBLE AT ANY MOMENT. . . . AN AGGRESSIVE MOVE BY JAPAN IS EXPECTED WITHIN THE NEXT FEW DAYS. . . . "

December 6, 1941 . . . President Roosevelt sent an unprecedented peace appeal directly to Emperor Hirohito, begging him to intervene in that eleventh hour to prevent disaster.

Early on December 7, 1941 . . . the answer to the frantic question "When?" appeared to reach Washington when a Japanese message was intercepted and decoded, directing the Japanese envoys to destroy their code machines immediately and break off negotiations at *precisely one o'clock* that afternoon, Washington time.

Washington's last war warning radiated out to San Francisco, Panama and the many Pacific Islands, emphasizing the ominous "one o'clock." Of all places, Hawaii was the only station not receiving. The signal officer could have tried two other direct lines, but chose instead to send a telegram. It arrived too late.

December 7, 1941, 7:55 A.M., Hawaii time . . . 353 Japanese planes flew in over the mountains of Oahu and attacked the naval base, where the U.S. Pacific fleet lay at anchor.

The surprise was total, the destruction horrifying. In a few hours the battleships *Arizona, Oklahoma, California* and *West Virginia* were sunk, the *Nevada* was run aground to prevent capsizing and the *Maryland, Tennessee* and *Pennsylvania* were all damaged. One hundred and eighty-eight planes were destroyed; 149 more mutilated. Over 2,400 American men were killed.

The news struck Americans like a thunderclap. Public attention had been focused so completely upon German U-boats in the Atlantic that the Japanese strike seemed like a "knife in the back" to a people caught looking the other way. The effect was electrifying. Americans were incensed at the deceit of a surprise attack and the murder of so many of their men on their own soil. They were suddenly, furiously and unanimously ready for total war.

Those were among the grimmest days in American history. Fascism reigned supreme on two huge continents, had made inroads in Latin America and was now threatening North America. Democracy appeared to be in retreat everywhere.

Germany and Italy followed the Pearl Harbor attack with their own declarations of war, and for the first time America was threatened from both oceans. German U-boats moved murderously into U.S. waters, patrolling the eastern seaboard and sinking an average of three ships a day, many within sight of the coast.

The Japanese rolled up victory after victory, capturing Shanghai, Guam, Wake Island, Hong Kong, the Malay peninsula, Singapore and the entire Dutch East Indies. They encountered their most stubborn opposition in the Philippines. There hundreds of thousands of Filipinos rallied to the side of the Americans and fought to the very end of their endurance. When their battered, starving and exhausted numbers finally crumbled early in May, 1942, the United States suffered the worst defeat in its history. Over 140,000 American and Filipino soldiers fell into the hands of the Japanese, who boasted that they would dictate peace terms from the White House.

America was totally unprepared for a war of such scope. In those early days she could not build ships as fast as they were being sunk. Eventually she swung into an unprecedented war production which astounded the world, but until then it was nip and tuck. The Philippine garrison fought to the end with obsolete World War I rifles and an air force of exactly two ancient patched-up fighter planes ("Dear Mr. President, our P-40 is full of holes; please send us another"), and the crucial Battle of Midway was waged with such lumbering antiques that some considered their pilots as "lost before leaving the ground."

The United States was saved by the courage and determination of its fighting men, who bought with their lives precious time for their country to lick its Pearl Harbor wounds and build for war. Many who lived through those dark days swore that they would never let America be militarily weak again.

It was a long, sweeping, ghastly conflict, but Americans united behind it 100 per cent. They knew exactly what they were fighting for—in Roosevelt's words, "a world in which this nation, and all that this nation represents, will be safe for our children." It was a bitter task, and there was no joy—merely a grim determination to see the ordeal through.

American casualties were painfully high. The total killed was quadruple that of World War I, and in one calculation—taking battle deaths alone—they even surpassed those of the Civil War (although, in terms of percentage of population, Civil War casualties would always remain unrivaled). World-wide losses were in the hundreds of millions. No estimate of civilian deaths has even been attempted (the war featured the saturation bombing of cities), although it is known that the German Government deliberately murdered about 8 million noncombatants, most of them Jews.

How could this horror have been avoided? By not permitting the "wicked" to rearm, according to Churchill, who felt that this had occurred through "unwisdom, carelessness and good nature." He thought that "there never was a war more easy to stop" and suggested that this most terrible of all world tragedies be called the "unnecessary war."

Even after Hitler rearmed, he could have been stopped—easily at the Rhine, with some casualties in Czechoslovakia. After

Czechoslovakia there was no way out but through the fire.
Then the nations of the world, including the United States,
were in the position of a schoolboy confronted by a bully. Like
it or not they had to fight.

There has long been a theory, popular in some quarters,
that President Roosevelt manipulated America into the war.
This distortion is based, in part, upon the fact that once Hitler
began to run rampant, Roosevelt's chief concern was not in
keeping the U.S. out of the war but, rather, in stopping Hitler.
To this end Roosevelt viewed America's entry as not only inevitable but actually desirable. Yet he was too well aware of the
country's military unpreparedness to expedite the moment.

Those who criticize Roosevelt's willingness to go to war
have lost sight of the fact that the United States really had no
choice. Not unless it was willing to see Hitler and Mussolini
convert all of Europe into a vast torture chamber and the
Japanese—whose treatment of a conquered people was medieval
at best—take over the Philippines and much of Asia. If Americans had acquiesced in all of this, what kind of a peace would
they have found in such a world? Surely sooner or later the
triumphant fascists, who were even then trying to develop
atomic weapons, would turn their attention to the Western
Hemisphere, and then the United States would have had to
fight almost alone.

It might very well have lost. As it was, it took three and a
half years, and the combined might of the United States, Great
Britain and Soviet Russia to bring Germany to her knees. And
the Soviet contribution was particularly enormous. In one of
his most insane moves Hitler had turned upon that country—
supposedly his ally—in June, 1941, launching a massive surprise attack along a 2,000-mile front. By the end of that year

his forces had pushed all the way to Leningrad and were converging on Moscow. In the process of dislodging these invaders from their soil—a process that took two years—the Russians inflicted upon the German army the worst disasters in all military history.

Even then the Germans fought to the bitter end. It was a replay of one of the greatest tragedies of war—the case of "my country right or wrong." Just as many Southerners who did not believe in slavery had rallied behind the Confederate flag, so did thousands of non-Nazis—even twelve-year-old boys—fight to the death for their homeland. Once war is brought to a man's doorstep, the issues that caused it cease to matter.

Nor was Japan an easy nut to crack. Here the United States bore almost the entire burden. The war in the Pacific was fought from island to island—the invasion of each island requiring amphibious landings, often against strongly entrenched positions. The Japanese dug in and bitterly contested every inch of ground. When they were finally pushed back, with horrendous casualties, they prepared to defend their homeland with the same suicidal determination. The invasion of Japan threatened to be a blood bath for all.

But a frightening new weapon made this invasion unnecessary. Americans had won the race with Nazi scientists to develop an atomic bomb, and now they used that deadly weapon twice on Japan to bring a quick end to what promised to be a lingering and gory nightmare.

The dropping of atomic bombs on Hiroshima and Nagasaki, with the resulting incineration of some 100,000 people, later became a matter of great controversy. But Winston Churchill expressed the feelings of most of the Allied world at the time: "To avert a vast, indefinite butchery, to bring the war to an end, to give peace to the world, to lay healing hands upon its tortured peoples by a manifestation of overwhelming power . . . seemed, after all our toils and perils, a miracle of deliverance."

Americans emerged from the rubble of World War II a sadder and wiser people. They were too chastened by events to talk of a "war to end all wars," but they were nevertheless grimly determined to somehow win the peace.

"The people of the United States did their best to stay out of European wars on the theory that they should mind their own business," Secretary of State James Byrnes explained in a speech in Paris. "It did not work. . . . They have concluded that if they must help finish every European war, it would be better for them to do their part to prevent the starting of a European war."

To that end they readily accepted not only membership but aggressive leadership in the United Nations, a world organization that would, it was hoped, be "ready and able to keep the peace, if necessary by force" (Roosevelt's words).

Alas, during the years that followed, America's determination to "keep the peace, if necessary by force" would lead to two more wars—neither even remotely approaching the dimensions of World War II, but major wars nevertheless.

X

Wars of Communist Containment

The seeds of the Cold War and its accompanying two hot ones—Korea and Vietnam—were sown during World War I and nourished by World War II.

World War I witnessed the jarring introduction of communism into the world community. World War II was a ghastly diversion, necessary to destroy the monsters that had risen in extreme opposition to communism. As such, it made strange bedfellows; the United States and Great Britain were allied with Soviet Russia.

This alliance was uneasy at best, held together by one thing only: a common enemy. When the enemy began to crumble, so did the alliance.

To the Western powers Russia was always, as Churchill said, "a riddle wrapped in a mystery inside an enigma."

185

Throughout the war Premier Josef Stalin remained aloof and suspicious, seldom revealing his plans or sharing vital information with his allies. He began to appear threatening when his armies, after driving the Germans from Russia, spread throughout central and eastern Europe. It soon became apparent that it might be impossible to dislodge them. Churchill and Roosevelt could not, after all, take from Stalin what his troops physically possessed—unless they wanted to start another war. They had to be content with Stalin's promise to conduct "free and unfettered elections" in those countries—a promise which, alas, he never kept.

Thus, even before World War II ended, new storm clouds were gathering. The unpleasant truth was that Stalin was as ruthless as Hitler; both were dictators in the same mold. Many Americans felt that as long as a man of this stamp held great power, the peace of the world was in danger.

They watched in horror as an "iron curtain" of communism descended across Europe "from Stettin in the Baltic to Trieste in the Adriatic," locking millions of unfortunate peoples under a new and brutal tyranny. As Churchill dramatically pointed out, "This is certainly not the liberated Europe which we fought to build up. Nor is it one which contains the essentials of permanent peace."

Even more alarming, all of Europe appeared in danger of falling under Russia's sway, for communism thrived on the poverty and misery that raged in the wake of war. At the end of World War II, Europe was in ruins. Churchill described it as a "rubble heap, a charnel house, a breeding ground of pestilence and hate." Its people, stalked by cold, hunger and disease, were in the depths of despair. Civil war with Communist forces broke out in Greece. Both Italy and France had strong Communist parties, possibly capable of staging a triumph. In a shocking *coup d'état*, Communists seized control of Czechoslovakia.

Stalin became increasingly more difficult. He threatened Iran, Turkey and Greece. He blocked all attempts to reunite Germany, sealing the eastern zone behind barbed wire and guns. He insisted upon his own reparations program, draining East Germany of its resources. In the United Nations his representatives were exasperatingly obstructive, sabotaging all efforts to establish some kind of international atomic control and organize a world police force.

On March 27, 1947, President Harry S. Truman formally recognized the existence of a rift between the United States and Soviet Russia. Every nation, he said, was faced with a choice between two ways of life. "One way . . . is based upon the will of the majority, and is distinguished by free institutions, representative government, free elections, guarantees of individual liberty. . . . The second way of life is based upon the will of a minority forcibly imposed upon the majority. It relies upon terror and oppression. . . . "

He in effect declared a "cold war" on the Soviet Union. Thenceforth U.S. policy would be to contain communism; it must not be permitted to spread any further. To this end America would "support free peoples who are resisting attempted subjugation," and concentrate on economic aid because "the seeds of totalitarian regimes are nurtured by misery and want."

The billions of dollars that the United States had already poured into Europe through loans, gifts, grants and relief organizations had barely staved off starvation and complete chaos. An enormous program was urgently needed, greater than any yet conceived.

Secretary of State George Marshall soon proffered just such

a program. He suggested that the European countries, including Russia and her satellites, draw up their own reconstruction plans and present them to the United States for financing. Russia denounced this "economic imperialism" and refused to participate, but the western European countries responded eagerly. They presented their needs, and on that basis President Truman asked Congress for an astounding $17 billion.

During the debate on this unprecedented peacetime request, Republican Senator Arthur Vandenburg, once an ardent isolationist, addressed his colleagues: "There are no blueprints to guarantee results. We are entirely surrounded by calculated risks. I profoundly believe that the pending program is the best of these risks. I have no quarrel with those who disagree, because we are dealing with imponderables. But I am bound to say to those who disagree that they have not escaped to safety by rejecting . . . this plan. They have simply fled to other risks, and I fear greater ones." The Senate passed the bill by a large majority.

This "Marshall Plan"—the greatest humanitarian program in world history—was an immediate and fantastic success. A tremendous influx of American money, food and equipment permitted Europe to begin a full-scale reconstruction. Within little more than a decade its economy was so restored that the balance of trade with the United States actually turned in Europe's favor. Today it is obvious that the Marshall Plan prevented at least some—and perhaps much—of western Europe from going into the Communist camp.

Meanwhile, Truman staunchly opposed all Communist aggression. When the Russians created a world crisis in June, 1948, by instituting a blockade around the city of Berlin—a city jointly occupied by all the major powers but located deep within the Russian zone—Truman refused to tolerate any suggestion (and there were some) that the western countries pull out of Berlin. "We are going to stay, period. There is no discussion on that point."

Recognizing that two million Berliners had been severed from all vital supplies, he directed an all-out effort to provision them by air. For almost ten months, as the threat of war hung heavy, hundreds of British and American planes ferried tons of food, fuel and other necessities into the city each day. The Berlin Airlift was a spectacular success. The Russians, after suffering a tremendous loss of prestige, finally lifted the blockade.

Incidents such as these impressed many Americans with the need to strengthen European defenses. "Unless Russia is faced with an iron fist and strong language another war is in the making," President Truman maintained. "Only one language do they understand—how many divisions have you?"

After considerable negotiation, the United States concluded the North Atlantic Treaty with fourteen European nations. This treaty, the most entangling alliance the United States had ever made, provided for the creation of joint military forces and committed the United States, with its nuclear power, to the active defense of all signatories.

"Experience has taught us that the control of Europe by a single aggressive unfriendly power could constitute an intolerable threat to the national security of the United States," Secretary of State Dean Acheson told the Senate. "It is a simple fact, proved by experience, that an outside attack on one member of this community is an attack on all members. We have also learned that if the free nations do not stand together

they will fall one by one." The lessons of World War II had
been well learned.

Not, however, by everyone. All of these actions, while supported by the vast majority of the American people, roused
heated opposition among some, who sincerely felt that the
United States was too belligerent and one-sided.

These people stressed America's colossal power. The United
States, after all, had emerged from World War II the wealthiest
nation in the history of the world. It was the only major country whose mainland had not been struck during the war,
whose industrial plant was totally intact. Furthermore, its
productive capacity had been expanded beyond the wildest
dreams. Its fleet was greater than the combined fleets of all
other nations in the world. Its global ring of strategic air bases
gave it a greater striking power than that of any other country.
In addition, it alone possessed the terrible atomic bomb.

The Soviet Union, in contrast, was gasping from her enormous war losses. Between fifteen and twenty million Russians
had been killed during the war. The Nazis had destroyed over
70,000 towns, 31,000 industrial plants, 55,000 miles of railway
track and 56,000 miles of major highway, converting fully
one-third of the country into a wasteland. Vast and victorious
though the Soviet Union was, she was in no position to challenge the might of the United States.

Indeed, the U.S.S.R. had every reason to fear America, whose
goals and ideologies directly opposed hers, and whose actions
appeared increasingly more unfriendly. America's position in
occupied Germany and Japan brought her frighteningly close
to Russia's borders. "How would it look to us if Russia had
the atomic bomb and we did not," Secretary of Commerce

Henry A. Wallace dramatically asked President Truman, "if Russia had 10,000-mile bombers and air bases within 1,000 miles of our coast lines, and we did not?"

What appeared to be Soviet expansionism was merely defensive policy, people like Wallace insisted. Russia, like any power, needed to maintain friendly nations on her borders.

And as for Russia's uncooperative behavior in the United Nations, that was clearly explained by her colossal distrust of the United States. Russia felt that the U.N. was an American-dominated organization rather than a true international body.

All of these arguments had some validity, and certainly the United States was often belligerent and unfair. However, from this distance one tends to be thankful that President Truman did not try to "understand" Stalin the way Neville Chamberlain had "understood" Hitler, for Stalin was far more unscrupulous than the American leaders, just as one-sided—if not more so—and certain to take undue advantage of any opportunity that came his way.

What the critics of American policy were missing was that while the United States was making mistakes, its basic goals and principles were less demonic than those of Stalinist Russia. This is clearly seen from an examination of the shocking political conditions under Stalin, the frantic exodus of millions of wretched people from his conquered countries and the general relief of much of the world that if there had to be a sole possessor of the atomic bomb, it was the United States and not the Soviet Union.

An objective view of those turbulent years recognizes the emergence from World War II of two opposing ideological blocs. The many incidents and crises can be attributed to the continual struggle of each bloc for power. This power struggle had been foreseen as early as 1830 by the brilliant French politician and writer, Alexis de Tocqueville: "There are at present two great nations in the world, which started from different points, but seem to tend towards the same end. I allude to the Russians and the Americans. . . . The principal interest of the [latter] is freedom; of the [former] servitude. Their starting point is different and their courses are not the same; yet each of them seems marked by the will of Heaven to sway the destinies of half the globe."

President Truman was determined to keep Russia's half as limited as possible. He did effectively clip Stalin's wings, and he won significant victories in the containment of communism.

He had his least success in Asia. There conditions were basically worse than in Europe, for the poverty and suffering of the people was centuries-old and shockingly widespread. American attempts to oppose the Communists in China's civil war failed completely, and in September, 1949, the Communists drove the Nationalists off the mainland and took over all of China. Thus one-fourth of the world's population was transferred into the Communist camp.

In Korea the United States encountered the same difficulties with Russia as in Europe. At the end of World War II, Stalin, honoring an earlier agreement with Roosevelt and Churchill, had declared war on Japan and sent his armies crashing into Manchuria and Korea (Korea then being possessed by Japan).

After the war Korea was jointly occupied by Soviet and American forces as a temporary expedient. The United Nations tried to reunite the country, but Russia blocked every move, and it remained arbitrarily divided along the 38th Parallel. In 1949 both the Russians and Americans withdrew

their troops, leaving in operation two opposing Korean governments—a Communist one in the North. Each government
ardently wanted to unify the peninsula under its own rule.

On June 25, 1950, without any warning, 70,000 North Korean
troops drove across the 38th Parallel and invaded South Korea.
To a world that remembered Japanese soldiers pouring into
Manchuria, Italian troops attacking Ethiopia and German
divisions crossing into the Rhineland, this rang a clear alarm
bell.

President Truman immediately brought the matter before
the U.N. Security Council. An unusual circumstance permitted
the Council to act: the Russians were temporarily absent, boy-
cotting the United Nations over its refusal to admit Red China
as a member. The Security Council promptly condemned the
North Korean action as a breach of peace and demanded
an immediate withdrawal of the North Korean forces to the
38th Parallel. It called on all member nations to "furnish such
assistance as may be necessary to repel the armed attack."

And therein lay the Korean War. Theoretically it was a
United Nations "police action" to enforce a Security Council
order. Actually, however, since the United States was best
equipped to send military aid, it was an American war—and a
serious one at that—to the dismay of the American people, who
only five years earlier had lost over 400,000 men in World
War II.

The United States furnished 48 per cent of the U.N. troops—
even more than South Korea, which supplied 43 per cent.
Fifteen other nations contributed the remaining 9 per cent,
many of which were only token forces.

The North Koreans overran the entire peninsula except for
the southern port of Pusan and a small perimeter before U.N.

forces, under the direction of General Douglas MacArthur, could launch a counteroffensive. MacArthur achieved brilliant success, driving the North Koreans back across the 38th Parallel and then—with U.N. permission—pursuing them into their own territory. Advance units almost reached the Red Chinese border when, at the end of October, 1950, hundreds of thousands of fresh Chinese troops suddenly poured across the Yalu River into Korea.

The U.N. forces reeled under this massive onslaught. General MacArthur called this "an entirely new war" and pleaded for permission to attack the Chinese at their source. United Nations delegates, however, feared that the entry of Red China might portend Soviet intervention. Since the Russians by this time also had the atomic bomb, World War III might be hanging in the balance. MacArthur was told to confine his operations south of the Yalu River. The war's objective was merely the enforcement of a U.N. order, and, therefore, the war had to be strictly limited.

This was very difficult for many Americans to understand. "Once war is forced upon us, there is no alternative than to apply every available means to bring it to a swift end," General MacArthur insisted. "War's very object is victory—not prolonged indecision. In war, indeed, there can be no substitute for victory."

When General MacArthur continued publicly agitating to extend hostilities to China, President Truman felt forced to dismiss him from command.

Bitter fighting raged up and down the Korean peninsula, and American casualties soared. There were many personal tragedies. Those were American boys, conscripted from civilian life, who were dying on those bleak Korean hills: Baldy, Pork

Chop, Bloody, Heartbreak, Sniper, Arrowhead. And, unfortunately, the disasters fell unevenly on the American people. Among other things, the type of airplane frequently required in the mountainous terrain necessitated the calling up of the only pilots trained to man them: World War II veterans, many of whom had flown a hundred missions over Germany or Japan. Those men had surely earned the right to pursue their own lives, yet in Korea their casualties were so high that many stood a fifty-fifty chance of being killed before they could return home. On the ground the loss among second lieutenants was notorious. The ranks of recent military school graduates were ravaged.

Even worse was the growing feeling that these men were dying in vain. American motives were being maligned by many Europeans, in whose interests, quite as much as their own, the sacrifices were being made. Americans, after all, wanted nothing from Korea; their only desire—and it was heartfelt—was for world peace.

The fighting finally settled down roughly along the 38th Parallel, and each side hammered at the other while negotiations began at Panmunjom. These talks were long and difficult. They were repeatedly broken off and then resumed. But finally, on June 27, 1953, the Communists agreed to withdraw their forces to the armistice line specified by the United Nations. Thus after three years the police action was a success. But at what a price! Americans had suffered 157,000 casualties, including 53,000 deaths. To many the bloodshed and heartbreak seemed to have accomplished nothing. Nothing had been won, nothing gained; the status quo had merely been restored.

This costly and frustrating experience filled many Americans with bitter misgivings. Their role as world leader was proving to be thankless and onerous.

However, as a whole, President Truman's three-point strategy for the containment of communism (a military, economic and alliance approach) was successful—so successful, in fact, that it was followed basically without change by Presidents Eisenhower, Kennedy and Johnson.

Thus, throughout the 1950s and 1960s, American policy. was based upon all the old, proven slogans: "The world must be made safe for democracy." "No more Munichs." "Force must be met with force." In crisis after crisis the United States stood firm, despite the fact that the Communists now possessed nuclear weapons and the threat of a world holocaust was ever-present—a holocaust in which hundreds of millions of people could be destroyed in a single hour and, in the words of Russia's Nikita Khrushchev, "the living would envy the dead."

The climatic event came with the Cuban missile crisis in the fall of 1962. When it was learned that the Soviets were building missiles on Cuba at a very rapid rate, President John F. Kennedy demanded an immediate dismantling of the bases and the withdrawal of all the missiles. The United States mobilized for war. For six nightmarish days, the world teetered on the verge of catastrophe. The United States and the Soviet Union were "eyeball to eyeball"; then Khrushchev "blinked." The missiles were removed from Cuba.

In this dramatic American victory, Khrushchev vividly learned that Americans were willing to fight to protect their vital interests. And Americans, in turn, learned that Khrushchev feared nuclear war as much as they did.

This was a crucial discovery. Seizing upon it, President Kennedy delivered an epochal speech at American University in June, 1963, recognizing that both the United States and the

Soviet Union "have a mutually deep interest in a just and genuine peace" and stressing "our mutual abhorrence of war." He suggested that we "direct attention to our common interests and the means by which [our] differences can be resolved. . . . For, in the final analysis, our most basic common link is that we all inhabit this small planet . . . and we are all mortal."

Departing strikingly from the fighting approach of Truman and Eisenhower, Kennedy insisted that Americans must "re-examine our attitudes." He declared that "we are . . . caught up in a vicious and dangerous cycle in which suspicion on one side breeds suspicion on the other." He took the old Wilsonian "The world must be made safe for democracy," which had so profoundly influenced American foreign policy for a quarter of a century, and modified it into the brilliantly sophisticated ". . . if we cannot end now our differences, at least we can help make the world safe for diversity."

This magnificent speech made a tremendous impact on the Soviet Union, opening doors that had long been closed. Since its delivery, Soviet-American thinking has grown steadily closer together (aided by a growing Soviet-Chinese rift), and the focus of the cold war has shifted to Asia.

In Asia, American attempts to contain communism have again erupted into a hot war, this time in the little country of South Vietnam, formerly a part of French Indochina.

The Vietnam War had no dramatic beginning like the Korean War, when thousands of soldiers suddenly launched an invasion. The cause of both wars was the same—a Communist attempt to take over the entire country. But in South Vietnam, this began insidiously, with guerrilla and terrorist activities.

And America's military involvement was extremely gradual. It occurred one step at a time—each step approved reluctantly but with the feeling that there was no alternative. Many people now feel that each step was taken without an intelligent appreciation of what was at stake, for each seemed to lead inevitably to another and a larger step.

Trouble had started in the Indochina area as early as 1946, when the people had revolted against the French. Fighting had dragged on for seven and a half years, during which time the rebel leader, Ho Chi Minh, repeatedly asked for American and U.N. intervention against French colonialism. He even requested President Truman to give Vietnam "the same status as the Philippines" for a period of tutelage before independence. But Ho was known to have "direct Communist connections," and his appeals were not answered.

In 1954, the French, despite generous American aid, were defeated. They managed to secure a negotiated settlement, known as the Geneva accords, which divided Indochina into the nations of Laos, Cambodia and Vietnam. Vietnam itself was further divided, with the Communists in the north, pending elections to determine the legitimate government of the country.

The Eisenhower Administration considered this Geneva settlement "a disaster . . . a major forward stride of communism." Following Truman's three-point strategy, it sponsored the Southeastern Asia Treaty Organization, pledging help to all member nations against "subversive actions directed from without," and initiated an urgent program of economic and military aid to South Vietnam.

The basic premise that communism should be opposed in Vietnam was not questioned; it was firm U.S. policy to oppose communism *everywhere*. Paramount was the "domino theory" —that if one nation fell to communism, another and then another would inevitably follow. The National Security Council believed that the "loss of any single country" in Southeast Asia would ultimately lead to the loss of all Southeast Asia and then India and Japan and finally "endanger the stability and security of Europe."

In its determination to "save Vietnam from communism," the U.S. Government felt obliged to support whatever government existed in opposition. American intelligence continually warned that the South Vietnamese leadership was shaky and unpopular and that this situation was "likely to deteriorate progressively." But Secretary of State John Foster Dulles, a rigid foe of communism, thought that "we have no other choice."

So the United States shored up the inefficient regime of Ngo Dinh Diem, which was riddled with corruption and so unresponsive to the needs of the people as to be outright brutal. "No organized opposition, loyal or otherwise, is tolerated, and critics of the regime are often repressed," according to one American intelligence report. Diem was responsible for a terrorist campaign which put from 50,000 to 100,000 people into detention camps and a land "reform" program which gave so much land back to the barons that by 1960 75 per cent of it was owned by 15 per cent of the people.

The war began initially as a South Vietnamese revolt against its own government. The Communists were quick to exploit the situation, however, infiltrating their own troops and gaining control. They won easy victories. When John F. Kennedy became president in 1961, Communist forces controlled much of the country. They virtually encircled the capital city of Saigon.

Diem began issuing urgent appeals for American combat troops and tactical air squadrons. Soon American officials were pressing for direct U.S. intervention.

Kennedy, like his predecessors, believed that the United States was engaged in a global conflict with communism. In his inaugural address he had promised that "we shall pay any price, bear any burden, meet any hardship, support any friend, oppose any foe to assure the survival and success of liberty." Kennedy decided that it was essential to prevent a Communist takeover of South Vietnam.

During his thirty-four months in office, he increased the American military "advisers" in Vietnam from 685 to roughly 16,000. This was accomplished so quietly that few Americans realized what was happening. A steadily growing casualty list —fourteen Americans killed in 1961, 109 in 1962 and 489 in 1963—finally alerted newsmen to the fact that at least some Americans were in combat situations. "Sir, what are you going to do about the American soldiers getting killed in Vietnam?" they asked at a White House press conference.

"We are attempting to help Vietnam maintain its independence and not fall under the domination of the Communists," Kennedy replied. "We cannot desist in Vietnam."

If Kennedy had lived, would he have continued that course, leading the United States into the all-out ground and air war that President Johnson pursued? There is no way of knowing.

The shocking assassination of Diem and his brother Ngo Dinh Nhu in November, 1963, following a coup that Kennedy had known about in advance and tacitly approved, could have been a turning point—especially since political conditions actually worsened after Diem's death, with governments rising and falling. "I saw the President soon after he heard that Diem and Nhu were dead," Arthur S. Schlesinger, Jr., later wrote. "I had not seen him so depressed since the Bay of Pigs." According to Schlesinger, Kennedy realized that at some point American intervention might "turn Vietnamese nationalism against us," converting an "Asian civil conflict into a white man's war."

Before he left for Dallas, Kennedy requested a plan for a total withdrawal of American forces by 1965. He indicated that he wanted a profound review of the entire Vietnam situation, including whether the United States should even be there at all.

But as all the world knows, President Kennedy did not return from Dallas. His successor, Lyndon B. Johnson, continued what Kennedy had started. That road led straight to the outright war that developed in 1965, for once the basic objective had been set, Vietnam became essentially a military problem. The determined pursuit of that ever-illusive goal—victory—invited continual escalation. Controversy among government officials during those years centered around strategy and tactics, not over whether the U.S. should even be in Vietnam at all.

The American people had virtually no control over these developments, although many were drafted to serve in the war that ensued. President Johnson did obtain a Congressional "Gulf of Tonkin Resolution" authorizing his actions, but few Congressmen, in passing this resolution, realized that the U.S. had been mounting secret provocative attacks against North Vietnam for months and was looking for an incident to justify the bombing of North Vietnam targets—a tactic that was appearing more and more desirable as the ground war became less and less successful.

As the war dragged on year after year with no end in sight, opposition began to mount at home. This opposition was slow in developing: at first the people trusted that their government knew what it was doing, and it seemed that many who opposed the war in the beginning were the same sorts who would have cheered Chamberlain after Munich. But when the American atrocity at Mylai was revealed, many responsible Americans began to feel that something was wrong—especially since their newspapers gave the impression that this was only one American atrocity of many. (The truth, according to many officers with an intensive firsthand knowledge of Vietnam, was that American atrocities were amazingly few, while Vietcong cruelty abounded. They maintained that newspaper correspondents were totally uninterested in Communist atrocities.)

American newspapers gave the impression that the war had degenerated into one of American soldiers against civilians, that it featured the ruthless destruction of hamlets and villages. More and more Americans, therefore, began to feel that the Vietnamese War contained the same basic fallacy as the Philippine Insurrection some sixty-five years earlier: that the only way of "liberating" the country was to destroy it. They began to wonder why the massive American military machine was *in* that tiny place 10,000 miles away, where the people had never even heard of Marx or Lenin and were merely struggling to feed their hungry children.

"A feeling is widely and strongly held that 'the Establishment' is out of its mind," an Assistant Secretary of Defense wrote Secretary Robert McNamara in May, 1967. "The feeling is that we are trying to impose some U.S. image on distant peoples we cannot understand . . . and that we are carrying the thing to absurd lengths."

By the beginning of the 1970s it was generally believed that some serious mistakes had been made—that the course which the U.S. Government had pursued was failing to accomplish its goals. Anger and frustration grew as many Americans began to feel that the Government was unresponsive to their views.

Dissension increased, bordering in some areas upon revolution.

More and more Americans began to demand an immediate termination of the war. "Boys, we all want this war to end," Senator Strom Thurmond of South Carolina stated, as he tried to soothe a group of protesting veterans at the Capitol, "but we want it to end in an honorable way." To which a one-armed ex-marine cried, "Senator, we ain't got any honor left."

"Each day . . . someone has to give up his life so that the United States does not have to admit something that the entire world already knows . . . that we made a mistake," an angry Vietnam veteran declared on NBC's "Meet the Press." "Someone has to die so that President Nixon won't be—and these are his words—'the first president to lose a war.'" Calling the Vietnam War "the biggest nothing in history," he cried, "How do you ask a man to be the last man to die in Vietnam? How do you ask a man to be the last man to die for a mistake?"

But how does a nation extricate itself from a "mistake" (and not everyone thinks it is a mistake), especially after the investment of so many years, money and lives? (The number killed in Vietnam exceeds American World War I battle deaths.) It is always easy for those without the responsibility (or all the facts) to demand extreme action. President Nixon—faced with all the practical aspects of the problem—elected to pursue a gradual withdrawal from the war.

An intelligent analysis of the Vietnam War will require a perspective of many years. It is impossible to appraise an event so recent. However, one fact remains incontestable: whether history will find the war justifiable or not, the American people gradually lost all heart for it. Mounting dissension at home undermined America's position at the bargaining table, leading the enemy to believe he would triumph in any event. The result, however viewed, is one of great disappointment for the United States.

This sad experience has forced many Americans to take a long, hard look at their country's role as world policeman. It has caused many to question the wisdom of continuing Truman's three-point strategy for the containment of communism. In a world that is changing as rapidly as ours, some people maintain, it is dangerous to adhere to any one policy for more than a few years. A nation that does not continually reassess its policies in the light of new developments may get into trouble.

The years after World War II were ones of great social and political upheaval. Old empires had crumbled, and many new nations were born. Revolutions against oppressive tyrannies were erupting. The Communists were quick to take advantage of such turmoil, and it became very difficult to distinguish between Communist and non-Communist activity. Thus the United States, in pursuing its policy of "Communist containment," gradually found itself opposing most revolutionary movements and supporting the status quo, however corrupt or tyrannical, simply because it seemed more stable. Rulers were able to manipulate the U.S. Government into financing their selfish ambitions merely by raising the threat of communism.

America's support for these repressive regimes made less and less sense as the world's population continued to increase geometrically and the problems of poverty grew more acute. Today billions of human beings are desperate to break the wretched pattern of their lives.

Direct economic aid (an important aspect of Truman's strategy) has failed to help them. In many cases the money falls into the wrong hands; corrupt officials become wealthy from funds intended for the poor. Sometimes the American Government and businesses work at cross purposes. Many nations feel that they are being economically exploited by American enterprises, which, they say, are siphoning more out of their countries than the U.S. Government is putting in. "For our people, monopolies are almost symbolic with the United States," a Brazilian archbishop explained, "taking the best of our natural resources." Many people maintain that the American "solution" to everything is just to pour in money. "More important than your money," the Brazilian insisted, "is your comprehension."

Comprehension of the peoples of Asia, Africa and Latin America seems urgent when one considers the sheer numbers at issue and the irrepressible emergence of this "Third World." A global civil war between the haves and the have-nots is not an impossibility. The elimination of social, political and economic inequality throughout the world—including the United States—has become the urgent need of the day.

In the face of these developments, the continued pursuance of "Communist containment" as the primary goal has often put the United States against the tide of human events. Many people think that a reassessment of American thinking is overdue. They suggest that we go back to World War II to reexamine our attitudes. After all, those who experienced the trauma of Nazism conquering Europe and menacing an unarmed United States, as well as the shock of a devastating surprise attack on Hawaii that came painfully close to mortally crippling the nation's Pacific defenses, can never forget.

Thus, in their mind, a brutal, ruthless Stalin was Hitler all over again, and the forceful expansion of communism was Nazism overrunning Europe. These impressions were strength-

ened by continual evidence of Communist brutality. When the
Soviet Union, and later Red China, obtained nuclear weapons,
the air raid sirens over Pearl Harbor began ringing in many
American ears. (The suggestion has been made that Stalin,
too, saw Hitler every time he looked at the United States.)

Americans dedicated themselves to the same uncompromis-
ing opposition they had shown to Hitler, but—especially after
Stalin's death in 1953—there were no more Hitlers around. In
their insecurity, Americans embraced the lessons of the past—
most particularly the one that taught that appeasement is fatal.
Even as late as 1971, President Richard Nixon was remember-
ing Neville Chamberlain returning from Munich "with his
umbrella" as a reason for tempering American withdrawal
from Vietnam.

This rigid adherence to lessons of the past has come up
against the fact that the present is simply different. By looking
backward, many American leaders have gradually lost touch
with reality. Many have failed to ask whether communism,
especially as it exists in the underdeveloped countries, really
has much resemblance to a nationalistic Hitlerism. Many have
assumed that when a nation "goes communistic," it automatically falls into the power camp of Russia or China. Few have
asked what even today is almost unaskable—whether perhaps
communism, after all, with all its faults, might not have its
place in this troubled world.

Among other things, communism contains the seeds of its
own destruction. The more the people are helped materially
by communism, the less enamored they become of its collectivis-
tic principles. Thus we have seen, with the increase of prosperity in the Soviet Union, the development of a middle class
which has had a moderating influence upon its government.

Perhaps this will someday happen in China. As John F. Kennedy said at American University, "The tide of time and events will often bring surprising changes in the relations between nations and neighbors."

The tide of time and events can work for a people, if they only keep abreast. This does not mean forgetting the lessons of the past but, rather, continually adjusting them to the conditions of the present. It would be a tragedy if we substituted "No more Vietnams" for the old "No more Munichs," or lost sight of the fact that communism has dangerous expansionist aspects, or forgot the vital lesson of World War II—that weakness invites aggression. It has been suggested that the lesson of Vietnam should be "No more easy slogans."

In a world racing toward the twenty-first century, continual growth and a firm grasp on reality are the vital keys.

Conclusion

The roads to war are many and varied, but some of their vehicles are the same.

For example, almost every war contains in one form or another the element of *change*. Generally speaking, one nation wants a change and another objects. Sometimes the change is natural or worthwhile or urgently needed; sometimes it is cruel and unjust. Sometimes those who cling to the status quo are selfish and shortsighted; sometimes the status quo should be defended at all costs. Often these disputes can be settled through negotiation, but when they can't, there is no higher authority to whom they can be appealed, and the issues are thrashed out on the battlefield. We live in a world where the mighty still prevail.

The successful negotiation of disputes is continually ham-

pered by a *lack of understanding, ignorance* and *wild emotion*
—threads that run through every war. These threads assume
every imaginable color and form. Self-deception is a common
one: nations, like people, seldom understand their true motiva-
tions. Little wonder, then, that they cannot grasp another's.
Blind spots prevail in abundance.

Hatred can sabotage all efforts for peace, and fear can para-
lyze the mind: this has been particularly true in the twentieth
century, when wars have become so horrible that each fosters
a rigid reaction to the one that has ended, severely hampering
all intelligent efforts to prevent the one that is developing.
Misinformation and sheer stupidity crop up again and again:
thus King George could not comprehend the nature of his
colonies, McKinley was full of misconceptions about the Filipinos and Hitler knew nothing about America (among other
things, he thought that Roosevelt was suffering from syphilitic
paralysis and was therefore mentally unsound).

People often do not even know their own countrymen. "We
are, I fear, within a few years of disunion and perhaps civil war;
and all because neither side knows the other," a Virginian
wrote in 1847. "Each has a hundred excellencies, entirely unknown to the other, and a knowledge of which would substitute mutual esteem if not mutual affections for the hate that is
now waxing bitterer and bitterer on both sides."

Today many white and black Americans do not understand
each other. The Arabs cannot understand the Jews. The Indians
cannot understand the Pakistanis. In Northern Ireland, the
Protestants cannot understand the Catholics, and vice versa.

Such understanding is frequently hampered by the existence
of an *injustice,* the elimination of which is essential for the
maintenance of peace. The American Civil War clearly showed

that a government cannot survive a basic evil. If wrongs are not corrected, they will sooner or later result in war.

Certainly wrongs will lead directly to *extremism*, one of the most dangerous spurs to war—one that often provokes the deadly course that can become irreversible. This was seen in America's Civil War, when the emergence of the Abolitionists shocked the South into an opposite position, one so rigid and untenable that hundreds of thousands of lives had to be sacrificed to effect the change that was long overdue. Prolonged extremism in any leadership is going to invite tragedy. It is wise, therefore, to keep moderate forces in control—men who can appreciate Abraham Lincoln's advice: "If both factions, or neither, shall abuse you, you will probably be about right."

As long as a nation is relatively free to do as it pleases, the nature of the man at the helm is of supreme importance. American history shows how leaders can control events. In recent times, the nature of the man in the White House has assumed even greater importance, for the president's war-making powers have greatly increased—a result of more efficient weapons of war and the urgent need for speed and secrecy in matters of national defense.

All of this is vastly complicated by the unpleasant fact that a nation living in a world jungle sometimes *has* to fight. There *is* such a thing as an unmitigated wrong, and as Lincoln said, "In a choice of evils, war may not always be the worst." There is a time to compromise and a time to put one's foot down— a time when an irresistible force has to be met by an immovable object.

This can be tragic, for in today's world it means the pitting of whole nations against each other, with so many other factors in the balance that hundreds of thousands of people who actually deplore the wrong have to fight to defend it. There is no way of removing an evil in a reluctant nation without crushing the nation altogether. Today the baby *has* to be thrown out with the bath water.

This will always be true until there is a higher authority with power to remove criminals like Adolf Hitler before they can fortify themselves behind huge armies—power to order nations to desist or change, for the good of all.

The ideal, of course, would be a world government such as Wilson envisaged; but such a government cannot be effective unless nations sacrifice some of their sovereignty to it. This is patently impossible as long as they distrust each other. Moreover, even if their suspicions were magically removed, the bowing to a higher authority would come very hard to nations long used to absolute independence. Many see such a move as a loss of freedom, not realizing that complete freedom (that is, every nation doing as it pleases) means no freedom at all; it means chaos, the law of the jungle, war. Liberty cannot exist without rules.

Even Americans, with their noble principles and traditions, have shown a need for rules. Certainly they were villainous in some of their previous wars. Many Americans have never come to grips with that part of their nature—conveniently forgetting it (the Philippine Insurrection has been all but erased from their reference books), glossing over it or convincing themselves that it could never happen now. Some people think that the Vietnam War has dramatized America's inability to be her own judge and jury. As Dag Hammarskjöld, former Secretary General of the U.N., once said: "We are on dangerous ground if we believe that any nation has a monopoly on rightness."

But even if the hurdle of national sovereignty were success-

fully passed, a world government would still face many problems. Consider the American Civil War, when two peoples
who spoke the same language and shared the same heritage
came to blows. If one of the greatest legal machines ever devised
by man, the United States Government, could split asunder,
then one wonders how a world federation could possibly succeed, embracing more than 140 nations, with extreme ideological, racial, economic, religious, cultural and language differences.

Yet "our problems are man-made," as John F. Kennedy told
the graduates of American University, and he insisted: "Therefore, they can be solved by man. . . . No problem of human
destiny is beyond human beings. Man's reason and spirit have
often solved the seemingly unsolvable—and we believe they
can do it again."   Indeed, history does reveal a certain progress
in the solving of this seemingly unsolvable problem. Men have
gradually learned to live together in larger and larger groups
until now they have actually leaped national boundaries. It is
unthinkable, for example, that Great Britain and the United
States, which twice came to blows, would ever make war on
each other again. And there is reason to hope that the United
States and the Soviet Union, which have never come to blows,
in fact never will.

But, as history clearly shows, this is not something that can
come naturally, without work or commitment. Rather, what
does seem to come naturally is war. It takes great effort to con-
struct and maintain the machinery under which men can live
in peace.

It is easy for individuals to feel powerless in the face of such
an overwhelming task, but the essence of hope and progress
lies in the belief that one person can indeed make a difference.

Thus Americans can strive to be informed, to learn more about other peoples, to correct (with intelligent understanding) the injustices that abound and to work for the election of excellent leaders. Each person can, in some small way, leave the world a better place than it was when he found it. That may not be very much, but the total can be significant.

There is an old Chinese proverb that a journey of a thousand miles begins with a single step. We may not live to complete the journey, but we can at least take our own small steps toward the rainbow—the golden moment envisioned by Isaiah when men "shall beat their swords into plowshares, and their spears into pruning hooks," when "nation shall not lift up sword against nation, neither shall they learn war any more."

SUGGESTED FURTHER READINGS

Space would not permit the listing of every reference used in the writing of *America's Wars—WHY?* The following is merely a list of books that are exceptionally readable, and should be of particular interest to young people.

I. On War
   Carr, Albert Z. *A Matter of Life and Death; How Wars Get Started or Are Prevented.* New York: The Viking Press, 1966.
II. The American Revolution
   Lancaster, Bruce, and the Editors of American Heritage. *The American Heritage Book of the Revolution.* New York: The American Heritage Publishing Co., 1958.
   McDowell, Bart. *The Revolutionary War: America's Fight for Freedom.* Washington: National Geographic Society, 1967.
   Montross, Lynn. *The Reluctant Rebels.* New York: Harper Press, 1950.
III. The War of 1812
   Tucker, Glenn. *Poltroons and Patriots,* vol. 1. New York: The Bobbs-Merrill Co., 1954.

IV. The Mexican War

Downey, Fairfax, and the Editors of American Heritage. *Texas and the War With Mexico*. New York: The American Heritage Publishing Co., 1961.

Lord, Walter. *A Time to Stand*. New York: Harper & Brothers, 1961.

Weinstein, Irving. *The War With Mexico*. New York: W. W. Norton & Co., 1965.

White, Owen P. *Texas: An Informal Biography*. New York: G. P. Putnam's Sons, 1945.

V. The Civil War

Catton, Bruce, and the Editors of American Heritage. *The American Heritage Picture History of the Civil War*. New York: The American Heritage Publishing Co., 1960.

Catton, Bruce and William. *Two Roads to Sumter*. New York: McGraw-Hill Book Co., 1963.

Oates, Stephen B. *To Purge This Land With Blood: A Biography of John Brown*. New York: Harper & Row, 1970.

Sandburg, Carl. *Abraham Lincoln: The Prairie Years and the War Years* (One-Volume Edition) New York: Harcourt, Brace & Co., 1954.

VI. The Spanish-American War

Brown, Charles H. *The Correspondent's War*. New York: Charles Scribner's Sons, 1967.

Weems, John Edward. *The Fate of the Maine*. New York: Henry Holt & Co., 1958.

VII. The Philippine Insurrection

Wolff, Leon. *Little Brown Brother; How the United States Purchased and Pacified the Philippine Islands at the Century's Turn*. Garden City, New York: Doubleday & Co., 1961.

VIII. World War I

Dos Passos, John. *Mr. Wilson's War*. Garden City, N.Y.: Doubleday & Co., 1962.

Marshall, Samuel L. A., and the Editors of American Heritage. *The American Heritage History of World War I*. New York: The American Heritage Publishing Co., 1964.

Smith, Gene. *When the Cheering Stopped: The Last Years of Woodrow Wilson*. New York: William Morrow & Co., 1964.

Tuchman, Barbara. *The Zimmerman Telegram*. New York: The Macmillan Co., 1958.

IX. World War II

Mosley, Leonard. *On Borrowed Time: How World War II Began*. New York: Random House, 1969.

Shirer, William L. *The Rise and Fall of the Third Reich*. New York: Simon & Schuster, 1960.

Sulzberger, C. L., and the Editors of American Heritage. *The American Heritage History of World War II*. New York: The American Heritage Publishing Co., 1966.

Post–World War II

Abel, Elie. *The Missile Crisis*. New York: J. B. Lippincott Co., 1966.

Fall, Bernard. *Street Without Joy: Insurgency in Indochina 1946–1963*. Harrisburg, Pa.: Stackpole, 1961.

Lederer, William. *A Nation of Sheep*. New York: W. W. Norton & Co., 1961.

INDEX

218

ABOUT THE AUTHOR

Elinor Goettel was born in Bangkok, Siam of American parents. Her father was in government service. She grew up in Washington, D.C. and graduated Phi Beta Kappa from Duke University, where she majored in history. In addition to her books for Julian Messner, she has written history articles for encyclopedias and scripts for documentary films. Her husband is a federal judge. The Goettels live in Rye, New York and have three children, Sheryl, Glenn and James.

Mrs. Goettel says: "This book grew directly out of a series of film strips which I compiled on American history. I found that I was most fascinated not by America's wars—for which there was an abundance of visual material—but rather by the stories behind America's entry into each war. I have long wanted to write a book presenting those ominous, tragic and often little-known events—so especially relevant today when war has become so horrible that its avoidance is of urgent concern to everyone. Julian Messner has given me this opportunity."